Shakespeare

Othello

A CASEBOOK

EDITED BY

JOHN WAIN

MACMILLAN

First published 1971
10th reprint 1989

Published by
MACMILLAN EDUCATION LTD
Houndmills, Basingstoke, Hampshire RG21 2XS
and London
Companies and representatives
throughout the world

Printed in Hong Kong

ISBN 0–333–07491–2 (paperback)

Gunman RONALD AYLING
John Osborne: *Look Back in Anger* JOHN RUSSELL TAYLOR

Pinter: *'The Caretaker' & Other Plays* MICHAEL SCOTT
Pope: *The Rape of the Lock* JOHN DIXON HUNT
Shakespeare: *A Midsummer Night's Dream* ANTONY PRICE
Shakespeare: *Antony and Cleopatra* JOHN RUSSELL BROWN
Shakespeare: *Coriolanus* B.A. BROCKMAN
Shakespeare: *Hamlet* JOHN JUMP
Shakespeare: *Henry IV Parts I and II* G.K. HUNTER
Shakespeare: *Henry V* MICHAEL QUINN
Shakespeare: *Julius Caesar* PETER URE
Shakespeare: *King Lear* FRANK KERMODE
Shakespeare: *Macbeth* JOHN WAIN
Shakespeare: *Measure for Measure* G.K. STEAD
Shakespeare: *The Merchant of Venice* JOHN WILDERS
Shakespeare: *'Much Ado About Nothing' & 'As You Like It'* JOHN RUSSELL BROWN
Shakespeare: *Othello* JOHN WAIN
Shakespeare: *Richard II* NICHOLAS BROOKE
Shakespeare: *The Sonnets* PETER JONES
Shakespeare: *The Tempest* D.J. PALMER
Shakespeare: *Troilus and Cressida* PRISCILLA MARTIN
Shakespeare: *Twelfth Night* D.J. PALMER
Shakespeare: *The Winter's Tale* KENNETH MUIR
Spenser: *The Faerie Queene* PETER BAYLEY
Sheridan: *Comedies* PETER DAVISON
Swift: *Gulliver's Travels* RICHARD GRAVIL
Tennyson: *In Memoriam* JOHN DIXON HUNT
Thackeray: *Vanity Fair* ARTHUR POLLARD
Trollope: *The Barsetshire Novels* T. BAREHAM
Webster: *'The White Devil' & 'The Duchess of Malfi'* R.V. HOLDSWORTH
Wilde: *Comedies* WILLIAM TYDEMAN
Virginia Woolf: *To the Lighthouse* MORIS BEJA
Wordsworth: *Lyrical Ballads* ALUN R. JONES & WILLIAM TYDEMAN
Wordsworth: *The Prelude* W.J. HARVEY & RICHARD GRAVIL
Yeats: *Poems 1919-35* ELIZABETH CULLINGFORD
Yeats: *Last Poems* JON STALLWORTHY

Medieval English Drama PETER HAPPE
Elizabethan Poetry: Lyrical & Narrative GERALD HAMMOND
The Metaphysical Poets GERALD HAMMOND
Poetry of the First World War DOMINIC HIBBERD
Poetry Criticism and Practice: Developments since the Symbolists A.E. DYSON
Thirties Poets: 'The Auden Group' RONALD CARTER
Comedy: Developments in Criticism D.J. PALMER
Drama Criticism: Developments since Ibsen ARNOLD P. HINCHLIFFE
Tragedy: Developments in Criticism R.P. DRAPER
The English Novel: Developments in Criticism since Henry James STEPHEN HAZELL
The Language of Literature NORMAN PAGE
The Pastoral Mode BRYAN LOUGHREY
The Romantic Imagination JOHN SPENCER HILL
Issues in Contemporary Critical Theory PETER BARRY

OTHER CASEBOOKS ARE IN PREPARATION

CONTENTS

ACKNOWLEDGEMENTS

S. T. Coleridge, 'Marginalia on *Othello*' and 'Report of a Lecture at Bristol', from *Shakespearean Criticism*, ed. T. M. Raysor (J. M. Dent & Sons Ltd, London, and E. P. Dutton & Co. Inc., New York); A. C. Bradley, extract from *Shakespearean Tragedy* (Macmillan & Co. Ltd); T. S. Eliot, extract from 'Shakespeare and the Stoicism of Seneca', from *Selected Essays* (Faber & Faber Ltd, London, and Harcourt, Brace & Co., New York); G. Wilson Knight, 'The *Othello* Music', from *The Wheel of Fire* (Methuen & Co. Ltd); William Empson, 'Honest in *Othello*', from *The Structure of Complex Words* (Chatto & Windus Ltd, London, and New Directions Publishing Corporation, New York); F. R. Leavis, 'Diabolic Intellect and the Noble Hero', from *The Common Pursuit* (Chatto & Windus Ltd, and New York University Press); Helen Gardner, 'The Noble Moor', from *Proceedings of the British Academy*, XLI (Oxford University Press); John Bayley, 'Love and Identity: *Othello*', from *The Characters of Love* (Constable & Co. Ltd); W. H. Auden, 'The Joker in the Pack', from *The Dyer's Hand* (Faber & Faber Ltd, London, and Random House Inc., New York); Nevill Coghill, extracts from *Shakespeare's Professional Skills* (Cambridge University Press).

GENERAL EDITOR'S PREFACE

Each of this series of Casebooks concerns either one well-known and influential work of literature or two or three closely linked works. The main section consists of critical readings, mostly modern, brought together from journals and books. A selection of reviews and comments by the author's contemporaries is also included, and sometimes comments from the author himself. The Editor's Introduction charts the reputation of the work from its first appearance until the present time.

What is the purpose of such a collection? Chiefly, to assist reading. Our first response to literature may be, or seem to be, 'personal'. Certain qualities of vigour, profundity, beauty or 'truth to experience' strike us, and the work gains a foothold in our mind. Later, an isolated phrase or passage may return to haunt or illuminate. Where did we hear that? we wonder – it could scarcely be better put.

In these and similar ways appreciation begins, but major literature prompts to very much more. There are certain facts we need to know if we are to understand properly. Who were the author's original readers, and what assumptions did he share with them? What was his theory of literature? Was he committed to a particular historical situation, or a set of beliefs? We need historians as well as critics to help us with this. But there are also more purely literary factors to take account of: the work's structure and rhetoric; its symbols and archetypes; its tone, genre and texture; its use of language; the words on the page. In all these matters critics can inform and enrich our individual responses by offering imaginative recreations of their own.

For the life of a book is not, after all, merely 'personal'; it is more like a tripartite dialogue, between a writer living 'then', a reader living 'now', and whatever forces of survival and honour link the two. Criticism is the public manifestation of this dialogue, a witness to the continuing power of literature to arouse and excite. It illuminates the possibilities and rewards of the dialogue, pushing 'interpretation' as far forward as it can go.

And here, indeed, is the rub: how far can it go? Where does 'interpretation' end and nonsense begin? Why is one interpretation superior to another, and why does each age need to interpret for itself? The critic knows that his insights have value only in so far as they serve the text, and that he must take account of views differing sharply from his own. He knows that his own writing will be judged as well as the work he writes about, so that he cannot simply assert inner illumination or a differing taste.

The critical forum is a place of vigorous conflict and disagreement, but there is nothing in this to cause dismay. What is attested is the complexity of human experience and the richness of literature, not any chaos or relativity of taste. A critic is better seen, no doubt, as an explorer than as an 'authority', but explorers ought to be, and usually are, well equipped. The effect of good criticism is to convince us of what C. S. Lewis called 'the enormous extension of our being which we owe to authors'. A Casebook will be justified only if it helps to promote the same end.

A single volume can represent no more than a small selection of critical opinions. Some critics have been excluded for reasons of space, and it is hoped that readers will follow up the further suggestions in the Select Bibliography. Other contributions have been severed from their original context, to which some readers may wish to return. Indeed, if they take a hint from the critics represented here, they certainly will.

A. E. Dyson

INTRODUCTION

Othello seems to have been written in 1604, and first performed at Court on 1 November of that year. It was printed in the First Folio in 1623, but there was a separate edition, in Quarto, brought out by one Thomas Walkley in 1622. Walkley presumably knew, by that date, that the First Folio, which offered a 'collected' Shakespeare to the public for the first time, was just about to appear, and perhaps rushed out his edition of the play to make a last-minute profit. But the text he used has several interesting differences from the one used by Heming and Condell. It omits 160 lines, adds a few and is not Bowdlerized; an Act of Parliament in 1606 forbade oaths on the stage, and the Folio text complies with this, but the Quarto does not, and perhaps goes back to an earlier manuscript. Editorial work on the text of the play has thus been full of problems from the beginning; the editor of the Second Quarto (1630) uses the First Quarto with some corrections derived from the First Folio.

For an editor, then, *Othello* has always been one of the most difficult of the plays, and to this day it bristles with unsolved textual problems and disputed readings. For the interpretative critic, on the other hand, it would seem to be one of the simplest of Shakespeare's major works. Compared with the dazzling complexities of *Hamlet*, the cloudy sublimities of *King Lear* or the delicate poetic symbolism of *A Winter's Tale*, there seems to be, in *Othello*, nothing much to dispute about. The play makes its terrific impact on us, we respond deeply or shallowly according to whether we have deep or shallow natures and there's an end of it. Or so, at least, I thought before I began the reading necessary for this book. Although the play had always been one of my favourites, I had not read much criticism of it, since I am one of those people who turn to criticism only when they feel themselves in difficulty. And with *Othello* I was conscious of no difficulty; I had a consistent interpretation of it which satisfied me.

I

Othello, as I saw it then and still see it now, is a tragedy of misunderstanding. No one among the characters understands anyone else; nor are they, for the most part, very strong on self-understanding either. If Othello understood Desdemona, he would know that she is simply not the kind of girl who would, during their very honeymoon, start a love affair with his first officer. If Desdemona understood Othello, she would know that he does not yet see her as a real girl, but as something magical that has happened to him, and that he will run mad if anything should happen to make him believe that her white magic has turned to black. If Emilia understood Iago she would know that he is not merely a coarsely domineering husband who has forced her into endless petty compromises for the sake of peace and a *modus vivendi,* but also, on a side hidden from her, a fiend who delights in torture. But then Iago does not, until it happens, know this about himself. Unaware of the power of love, he cannot imagine the suffering into which he will plunge Othello by plausibly slandering Desdemona, and therefore cannot imagine the holocaust at the end. Nor can he foresee the transformation that will occur in himself. The great temptation scene (III iii) is so convincing because it shows Iago's fall as well as Othello's. At the beginning of that scene they are both sane men; at the end, they are both mad, and both in the grip of the same madness. Hence the dreadful tragic irony of

– Now art thou my lieutenant.
– I am your own for ever.

Iago, the matador, succumbs to the excitement of his combat with the bull. One mistake, and those deadly horns will rip him to pieces. From that point on, he abandons all thought of motives and works from contingency to contingency. Of course Desdemona must die, for if she lives it will come out, one day, that Iago was lying, and Othello will hunt him down if it takes the rest of his life. Cassio must die for the same reason. Likewise Roderigo, who also knows too much. (And, like everyone else in the play, understands too little.) Iago's original intention, however much he may dress it up in a patchwork of motives, is to do as much harm to Othello and Cassio as his stunted little imagination can suggest. That harm turns out to be as far beyond his original conception as Othello's love for Desdemona is beyond his vulgarian's notion of love as 'a lust of the blood and a permission of the will'. Once he realizes the gigantic suffering he has unleashed, and the destructiveness that goes with it, he cannot halt or even slow down: it is too late. But Iago continues on course for reasons other than self-preservation. He is intoxicated; he has bull-ring fever. He is the perfect type of all those insignificant little men – they turn up every week, in the murder cases – who all at once feel the urge to destroy another human being, and get drunk on the realization that this large, important action is suddenly, incredibly, in their power.

II

If this view is correct, and *Othello* is a tragedy of misunderstanding, how does this arise? Why do the characters misunderstand each other? In each case, Shakespeare has provided, it seems to me, a sufficient answer. Desdemona, already young and inexperienced, has been over-protected by her father, so that she has even less knowledge of life and people than she might have. Iago misunderstands because, when it comes to anything that concerns the more generous emotions, he is a brute and a fool. Roderigo misunderstands because, in any case rather stupid, he is persuasively misled by Iago. Othello is taken in by Iago not only because Iago is a good actor (a fact which Shakespeare has already planted in II i) but because Iago has previously shown himself trustworthy and is so regarded by everyone; and also because, for all his power and importance in Venice, he is an outsider. Venice needs him, uses him, rewards him, but does not entirely take him in. His acceptance is partial; there are certain limits to it, which, though they are not spoken of, are quite clear in everyone's mind. Brabantio, to take the most notable example, has been glad to have Othello as a guest in his house, has in fact 'loved' him, but feels betrayed when Othello marries his daughter. (The justification for Othello's and Desdemona's secrecy, for the clandestine wooing and midnight elopement, is obviously that if Othello had asked in a normal way for Desdemona's hand in marriage, Brabantio would have refused, forbidden him the house as he had already forbidden Roderigo, and thereafter had the girl watched day and night.)

This, of course, raises the question of Othello's colour. I agree with Mr Louis Auchincloss that Othello is not regarded by the aristocratic Venetian characters as a social inferior: 'They regard him as Victorian Englishmen might have regarded some splendid Maharajah. . . . The Venetian aristocrats will not admit him to their inmost society, and they certainly do not want their daughters to marry Moors. But then they probably would not marry their daughters outside of fifty families along the Grand Canal.'[1]

Still, Brabantio thinks his daughter must have been bewitched to make her want to do anything as 'unnatural' as marrying a black man, and throughout the play the characters who dislike Othello tend to make it an additional point against him that he is a Negro. Those who like him tend to make no fuss about his colour one way or the other; while there is nobody, however pro-Othello, who says that he is all the more admirable *because* of his race, for the early seventeenth century had not heard of 'negritude'.

Those who fall under the spell of Othello's personal magnetism, who see, as Desdemona puts it, his visage in his mind, do not find anything unattractive in his racial characteristics. In the murder scene Desdemona does indeed find him terrifying as he rolls his eyes and gnaws his nether lip, details which seem to be hints to the actor to play the scene like a full-blooded African; but, since he is about to murder her, the poor girl might be forgiven for being frightened of him. What is important about Othello's racial difference from the other characters is not that it makes him terrifying or disgusting – it manifestly doesn't, except to people with a grudge against him already – but that it is the outward symbol of his isolation. Throughout the play, whether in the close-knit social fabric of Venice, or in the garrison-town atmosphere of Cyprus, he is surrounded by people who are different from himself in every way, just as he was on that far-off day that comes back to his mind in the last few seconds of his life, when in the Turkish city of Aleppo he intervened to protect a visiting Venetian businessman who was being beaten up in the street: a street full of people whom he chose to defy and dominate, whereas the Venetians were people he had chosen to serve. In each case it was a *choice*, a conscious decision of the will, not the blind natural instinct that makes a man fight for his own hearth and his own gods. Othello willed himself into a relationship with Venice, and the will is terribly limited in what it can achieve. Hence his insecurity; hence his touching pride in the way he has carried out his side of the bargain ('I have done the state some service'); hence the fact that Desdemona's love, which gives him an intimate, living link with Venice and promises to break down his outsiderdom, is central to his whole being, so that when he thinks it withdrawn he despairs of going on with *anything*, even his trade of fighting ('Othello's occupation's gone'); hence his bewilderment before Iago's commonplace cunning, the bemused suffering of the bull in the bull-ring.

III

Such were my thoughts about *Othello*; and, serenely reading and watching the play according to these notions, I imagined that the critics, when I came to study them, would on the whole, and with modifications here and there, give support to the interpretation I found so unquestionable. Far from it. What awaited me was the usual experience that comes to one who reads criticism in bulk. It was like walking placidly down a quiet corridor, opening a door and suddenly coming upon a crowd of people arguing at the tops of their voices. One faction was praising Othello, attributing to him a generous share of every virtue under the sun; another was busily destroying his character, offering a view of him as a coarse, vain, lustful and brutal ruffian who would be very apt, Iago or no Iago, to murder his wife on some delusory grounds. Hands were held up in horror at the wickedness of Iago, some of those most shocked professing at the same time an involuntary tremor of admiration at his unsurpassed brilliance and the coolness of his villany; in another corner, he was dismissed as a mere creature of the plot, a shallow liar and braggart who could never have taken in anyone less stupid and self-centred than his master. Others, again, dwelt on his wrongs and murmured that revenge was, after all, a kind of wild justice. At the mention of Desdemona's name, some eyes filled with tears of pure adoration; others became narrow and suspicious. Not only the characters, but the play as a whole, came in for totally different interpretations. The idea of magic is central to it.[2] The idea of magic is not central to it.[3] It is a Christian tragedy – Othello's fall is a version of Adam's, while the fate of Desdemona is an inversion of Eve's.[4] Its plot is incredible.[5] Its plot has 'surrealistic rightness'.[6] It is part of the response to James I's heroic poem, 'Lepanto'.[7] It is a diagram of Spanish political history, with Othello as Philip II and Iago as his enemy, Antonio Perez.[8] 'Perhaps the greatest work in the world', trumpets one voice;[9] but another growls, 'A bloody farce without salt or savour.'[10]

The character of Othello himself has provided a focus for ramified disagreement. To Swinburne, Othello was 'the noblest man of man's making'; T. S. Eliot, on the other hand, spoke rather sourly of his 'cheering himself up' and came out with that celebrated critical *mot* about 'Bovarysme'. And the dispute goes on. Nevill Coghill, in these pages, shows convincingly that Eliot's view could never be convincingly manifested by an actor and is therefore unlikely to have been intended by a consummate dramatic artist like Shakespeare; on the other side, Robert B. Heilman comes very close to restating the Eliot position when he says:

> Othello is the least heroic of Shakespeare's tragic heroes. The need for justification, for a constant reconstruction of himself in acceptable terms, falls short of the achieved selfhood which can plunge with pride into great errors and face up with humility to what has been done. All passion spent, Othello obscures his vision by trying to keep his virtues in focus.[11]

The classic inheritor and developer of the Swinburne line is A. C. Bradley; of the Eliot line, F. R. Leavis. In their respective essays, the two possible attitudes towards 'the noble Moor' stand revealed without qualification or misgiving. To read the two essays together, and try to achieve some mediation or synthesis between them, is a fascinating critical exercise. For the disagreement affects, as it is bound to, every facet of the play and every character. Since Bradley takes Othello to be entirely blameless, he has to explain why anyone should hate him so much as to destroy him. He accordingly sites the main complexity of the play within Iago's character, and devotes about half of his total space to an analysis of it, conducted with that characteristic Bradleian scrupulousness and intensity. To Dr Leavis, this preoccupation with the inner reaches of

Iago's mind is hardly more than a simple waste of time; as he sees it, Iago, though 'sufficiently convincing as a person', is 'subordinate and merely ancillary ... not much more than a necessary piece of dramatic mechanism'. Othello's tragedy, to Leavis, is essentially precipitated by Othello's own shortcomings – by his egotism, and by his love of Desdemona which is merely sensual and possessive and does not extend to any real knowledge of who and what it is that he is loving. ('It may be love, but it can be only in an oddly qualified sense love of her'.) To Leavis, Othello's habit of self-idealization, his simple heroic way of seeing himself in wide-screen images, served him well enough in a life of martial adventure, but would never have fitted him for the reciprocity of marriage, so that 'the tragedy is inherent in the Othello–Desdemona relationship'. When things go wrong, when pressure builds up, Othello's inadequacies are revealed like the cracks in a dam. 'The self-idealization is shown as blindness and the nobility as here no longer something real, but the disguise of an obtuse and brutal egotism.'

Leavis's view would make the play largely a criticism of Othello's character. Certainly it is true that Othello's blindness, his vulnerability to Iago's suggestions, arise from that statuesque largeness of outline which makes him unwieldy in manoeuvre. He *is* an egotist; we see it in his coolly callous treatment of Brabantio, or in the account of his wooing which he gives to the Senators – an account which makes it sound as if *she* wooed *him*, and doesn't at all square with Desdemona's later protestation that Cassio

> came a-wooing with you, and so many a time,
> When I have spoke of you dispraisingly,
> Hath ta'en your part.

Othello's life has not been such as to allow him the luxury of fine discrimination and *nuance*. Since his arms had seven years' pith, he has lived in an atmosphere where to hesitate, to have second thoughts or inner reservations, was to be killed by enemies who were prepared to be simple and decisive. Such a life breeds egotists. And Othello's egotism is egregious enough to make Iago's work fairly easy.[12] But to say this and to wash our hands of him, to echo Leavis's 'the essential traitor is within the gates', is to dodge the emotional impact of the play, to deny somehow that the tragedy is tragic. And this, surely, falsifies the experience we can testify to having undergone. We know that we have witnessed the overthrow of a strong and generous man; our hearts have been wrung as they would not have been wrung by the sight of a preposterous egotist (whatever his countervailing good qualities) getting his deserts. To me, Bradley is closer to the heart of the play, for all his over-elaboration and his side-issues; he recognizes that the tragedy lies in the assassination of love by non-love; he may go on too much about Iago, but he understands the essential truth about him, that he was less than a complete human being because love had been left out of his composition, left out so completely that he did not recognize it or suspect its existence. (Even Roderigo, who perceives very little, understands things that Iago does not understand; he knows that Desdemona is 'full of most blessed condition'; he loves her, and his love instructs him in her true nature.) Bradley puts it very well: '[Iago] was destroyed by the power that he attacked, the power of love; and he was destroyed by it because he could not understand it; and he could not understand it because it was not in him.' Othello, egotist as he is, unpractised at understanding other people as he is, retains the possibility of development because he knows what it is to love. And it is only the loveless heart that cannot learn.

Leavis's view, then, seems to me a brilliant (and characteristically trenchant) account of what Othello *is*; but Shakespeare's tragedy is tragic because it takes account, by implication, of what Othello *may become*; and this too Bradley sees, when he tells us that Othello in middle age 'comes to have his life crowned with the final glory of love'. Part of that crowning, we are surely meant to perceive, would be the easing of Othello's rigid stance towards life, the diminution of his egotism in the joy of knowing and loving another person.

IV

However that may be, Leavis and Bradley represent the two principal ways in which the character of Othello, and consequently the tragedy, have been viewed. With regard to Iago, they agree at least in finding him repulsive. Whether on a large scale or a small scale, he *is* the villain, the 'demi-devil'. And yet, it seems, even Iago has had his apologists. As early as 1790, a 'Gentleman of Exeter' published an essay called 'An Apology for the Character and Conduct of Iago', based on the incontrovertible fact that Iago has a good reputation, as man and soldier, before the story opens, and arguing that if he were really wicked it would surely have been noticed in his twenty-eight years. In the nineteenth century two critics, the Englishman Heraud and the American Snider, found themselves believing that Iago has actually been cuckolded by Othello; this would give him a powerful motive for revenging himself, and thus make his conduct, though still wicked, that of a man and not a mysterious fiend. Several twentieth-century critics have followed these two in finding Iago's suspicion a reasonable one; John W. Draper, after assembling satisfactory evidence that Elizabethan notions of honour made the cuckold a universally despised figure and that any man threatened with this fate would understandably seek his revenge, asks: 'Is Iago then so black a villain? Is he not a commonplace Renaissance soldier, "honest as this world goes", caught in the fell grip of circumstance and attempting along conventional lines to vidicate his honour? Indeed, if honesty and honour be something of the same, is he not from first to last "honest Iago"?'

Even if we find it incredible (as I do, for one) that

Othello has, at some earlier stage, made love to Emilia, there remains the fact that Iago thinks he may well have done, and thinks, moreover, that a lot of people believe he has ('it is thought abroad that 'twixt my sheets He has done my office'). Whether Iago has any grounds for this suspicion or whether he is just being neurotic, the belief is strong enough to 'gnaw his inwards' like 'a poisonous mineral', so that in one of his later soliloquies (III iii), when he is rejoicing in the torment he is causing Othello, he can revert to the same imagery and say,

> Dangerous conceits are in their natures poisons
> Which at the first are scarce found to distaste
> But, with a little act upon the blood,
> Burn like the mines of sulphur,

and know what he is talking about. On this view, his motive would be to make Othello go through the same agony as himself. Thus Mario Praz, who sees Iago as 'incensed by the public report that Othello has cuckolded him', points out that the story of his revenge has 'parallels in many cases of retaliation instanced by Italian *novelle*'.

Once more a polarity reveals itself; as in the case of Othello, critics divide into two camps. On the one hand there are those who take it that Iago does not really understand his own motivation, and when he claims to do so, in his soliloquies, he is merely rationalizing. Coleridge's phrase, 'the motive-hunting of a motiveless malignity', is much quoted in this camp. Hazlitt, a little later, saw Iago in a similar light, as an aesthete of evil. He denies that Iago is without motivation, for 'Shakespeare . . . knew that the love of power, which is another name for the love of mischief, is natural to man. He would have known this . . . merely from seeing children paddle in the dirt or kill flies for sport.' To Hazlitt, Iago is 'an amateur of tragedy in real life; and instead of employing his invention on imaginary characters or long-forgotten incidents, he takes the bolder and more desperate course of getting up his plot at home, casts the principal parts among his nearest friends and connections, and rehearses it in downright earnest with steady nerves and unabated resolution'. (My own view, that his immediate motives for hostility are clear enough but that the full range of possibilities only comes into view with action, and calls out an unexpectedly fiendish side to his own nature, clearly makes me a satellite of this critical body.) On the other hand there are the critics who see Iago's motives rather as he professes to see them himself. To Kenneth Muir, 'The secret of Iago is not a motiveless malignity, nor evil for evil's sake, nor a professional envy, but a pathological jealousy of his wife, a suspicion of every man with whom she is acquainted, a jealous love of Desdemona which makes him take a vicarious pleasure in other men's actual or prospective enjoyment of her at the same time as it arouses his hatred of the successful Moor and, it may even be suggested, a dog-in-the-manger attitude that cannot bear to think of Desdemona happy with any man, and especially with a coloured man, a man he hates.'[13]

V

To my mind, the most successful of the attempts to mediate between these two schools is the strenuous chapter on 'Honest in *Othello*' in William Empson's *The Structure of Complex Words* (1951). The gist of this chapter is reprinted here, but readers should note that the argument is much easier to follow if it is put back in the context of the book. A word is 'complex' when it has a cluster of possible meanings, the smaller ones not so much fighting the 'head sense' as sheltering under it and taking on its protective colouring so as to live their own lives in safety. To interpret a complex word correctly is to understand fully the passage, and often the whole work, in which it occurs. Clearly this kind of criticism, though its procedures are 'verbalist', is no mere matter of lexicography or semantics: it is concerned with sorting out feelings, and life-styles, and social attitudes (different senses of a word tend to be dominant among different classes).

Mr Empson gets to work on 'honest' with two richly suggestive chapters on the development of the word from its mediaeval use ('deserving the receiving social honour'). About the middle of the sixteenth century, he traces the beginning of a vague slang use for purposes of general approval among friends. An 'honest' man came to mean 'one of us, the type we like'. Since the simpler and older Chaucerian sense might now have unintentionally comic undertones, it quickly died off, leaving a new 'head sense': 'truthful, not stealing, promise-keeping'. The contrapuntal play of these two senses gave scope for irony, since an 'honest' man, one who owned up to his motives, however discreditable, might be selfish and unreliable and yet 'honest' in the sense of not being a hypocrite, therefore truth-telling. This alternative sense became very powerful during the Restoration, with its anti-Puritan feeling and its cult of (especially aristocratic) independence. One has the impression, in fact, that the use of 'honest' to mean 'one of us' travels upwards from the lower to the upper classes during the seventeenth century. (Certainly if Shakespeare caught it at the moment when it began its upward trajectory he could use it to convey a great deal of the range of feeling of someone as touchy as Iago.)

Empson continues his biography of the word 'honest' until he reaches the wonderfully rich but stable cluster of meanings indicated by this passage:

> A Victorian gentleman, while Gladstone was being discussed, could remark (in his pompous manner) 'honest Jones, our butcher, thinks the man a windbag', and this could chiefly mean that he was himself in doubt. Gladstone might be above Jones's head, or Jones might have sturdy common-sense: in any case what you needed here was a certain breadth. A slow and rather dumb readiness to collect the evidence, a

quality that Jones probably has, is in view, however much Jones may be a fool.

Armed with this kind of insight, Mr Empson proceeds to interpret the character of Iago, and his function in the play, by means of the reverberations of the word 'honest' as he applies it to himself and has it applied to him by others. His essay is in fact a close and sensitive piece of character-analysis, almost Bradleian, though in a very different idiom from Bradley's; it shows us an Iago who is certainly wicked and not to be defended, but also human and credible. Iago's class-jealousy is alerted by the patronizing overtones in the word 'honest'; he feels, probably quite rightly, that Cassio was important to Othello in a way that he could never be – notably as an intermediary in Othello's wooing – and this led directly to Cassio's being promoted over his, Iago's, head; so that Cassio, in addition to being 'a mathematician' (i.e. better educated), is also a charmer who is unfairly rewarded for his gentlemanly manners. This same plausibility is the reason why Iago fears Cassio with his nightcap, as well as Othello, and gives him a powerful set of motives for trying to bring the two of them into collision. Empson's account also offers us an Iago who is 'honest' in the sense that, for a surprising amount of the time, he really is uttering his true opinions, and one of the things that irritate him is the way people always assume, when he comes out with some misanthropic remark, that it is only his fun, whereas his cynicism really does have roots deep in his destructive emotions.

To me, Mr Empson's essay is the most fruitful of all interpretations of the play since Bradley's, and I find it rather dismaying that Dame Helen Gardner, in her wise and beautiful essay, should suddenly turn and give Empson a kick in passing (see p. 155). The fragment she quotes is not, in fact, central to Empson's interpretation and fails entirely to convey its complexity and richness; it is taken from a third and rather tailing-off section of his chapter, not reprinted here, in which he seems to be talking to himself after a spell of reading what other critics have said, and wondering aloud whether his interpretation can, or cannot, be squared with theirs. And even in that section he says that in the stage interpretation of Iago 'something very like a devil is what is wanted; a performance should not soften the character but manage to make us accept it when it is played all out as both wicked and coarsely funny'.

And so the theories of Iago's character mount up, until one is reduced once again to that bewildered and yet exhilarated condition in which one exclaims that Shakespeare's work has the baffling richness of life itself. The list of interpretations could be extended, but perhaps one more is enough. In 1938, Laurence Olivier played Iago, opposite the Othello of Ralph Richardson, as a repressed homosexual whose motive was an unrecognized passion for Othello. The production was not a success, largely, one gathers, because most people in the audience could not make out what Olivier was supposed to be conveying; but the theory itself marched on, and was given a full-scale exposition by a writer in the *Psychoanalytical Quarterly* in 1950.

VI

And Desdemona? Surely there is agreement about her? Bradley, for his part, is unashamedly a worshipper: 'Desdemona, the "eternal womanly" in its most lovely and adorable form, simple and innocent as a child, ardent with the courage and idealism of a saint, radiant with that heavenly purity of heart which men worship the more because nature so rarely permits it to themselves...' It is true, he admits, that she is not clever; where an earlier critic, Mrs Jameson, had credited her with 'less quickness of intellect and less tendency to reflection than most of Shakespeare's heroines', but thought she made up for it by having 'the unconscious address common in women', Bradley says firmly that Desdemona 'seems deficient in this address, having in its place a childlike boldness and persistency, which are full of charm but are unhappily united with a certain want of perception'. No doubt he considers it part of Desdemona's innocent childishness that she is inclined to be economical with the truth. Heraud in 1865 had already noted that 'Her passion was romantic, and there exists fiction in whatever is romantic. She suffers from illusion and loves to be deluded. If she is self-deceived, she likewise deceives others.... From timidity of disposition she frequently evades the truth, when attention to its strict letter would raise difficulties.'

If Heraud was strict, John Quincy Adams, sixth President of the United States, had already been far stricter. To him, Desdemona was little better than 'a wanton':

> Her conversations with Emilia indicate unsettled principles, even with regard to the obligations of the nuptial tie, and she allows Iago, almost unrebuked, to banter with her very coarsely on women. This character takes from us so much of the sympathetic interest in her sufferings, that when Othello smothers her in bed, the terror and the pity subside immediately into the sentiment that she has her deserts.[14]

I am a Bradleian here; what Desdemona reveals in the 'willow' scene with Emilia is, to me, a touching innocence about sexual matters, accentuated in the presentation by the fact that Othello's brutality has left her in a state of shock in which she has sought refuge in the pre-pubertial emotions. I suppose what the President meant by that remark about her 'unsettled principles' is that she asks Emilia in a wondering tone if it is really true that some women break their marriage vows, instead of simply stamping her foot and refusing to hear about it; and also because, in a kind of free-association way, she brings in the name of Lodovico and says he is 'a proper man'. Mr W. H. Auden seizes on the same point: in this scene, he says, Desdemona

> . . . speaks with admiration of Ludovico and then turns to the topic of adultery. Of course, she discusses this in general terms and is shocked by Emilia's attitude, but she does discuss the subject and she does listen to what Emilia has to say about husbands and wives. It is as if she had suddenly realized that she had made a *mésalliance* and that the sort of man she ought to have married was someone of her own class and colour like Ludovico.

These interpretations would not, I think, stand up to stage production. It would be very difficult to get the actress playing Desdemona to render her wandering, shocked, child-like remarks about adultery as a 'discussion'. Or to convey that she thinks of the ruin of her Eden as something merely unsuitable, a 'mésalliance'.

VII

I found, then, that there was a great deal of disagreement about this apparently straightforward play, and that much of it was relevant, perceptive debate and not mere argufying. In fact, *Othello* has been the subject of lively dispute ever since its own century. Thomas Rymer's amusing and pugnacious *A Short View of Tragedy* (1693) gave the play a hostile scene-by-scene analysis, rejoicing in every improbability, and generally seeing it as a compendium of faults. The whole performance is too long for inclusion here, but we join him as he begins on Act IV and follow him to the end. This, at least, gives the flavour of Rymer's ferocious cross-examination (he was a lawyer who studied the drama as a hobby); merely to quote his general conclusions about the play, as most selections do, is to make him look a fool, and he was actually a sharp-witted man with an axe to grind. English drama, in the last years of the seventeenth century, stood at an important cross-roads; the period of silence during the Commonwealth, when the theatres were closed by law, had been long enough to obscure the tradition that flourished from the days of Elizabeth to those of Charles I. There was no particular reason why the English drama should revert to its old ways, and Rymer was for starting again with a truly 'classical' theatre that should rival the French. To do this it was necessary to get rid of Shakespeare, whose plays, old-fashioned as they were, continued to fill the theatre and thus keep Elizabethan conventions alive in the minds of audiences. *Othello*, on Rymer's own admission, was a great favourite, so he turned all his guns on it, as Tolstoy was later to do, from not dissimilar motives, on *King Lear*. Of the two pieces of monumental wrong-headedness, I prefer Rymer's, which is at least amusing and, in its own way, very acute.[15]

Rymer finds the plot of *Othello* incredible. (Some of his objections turn up again in an essay by Robert Bridges, written in 1906 and published twenty years later.)[16] He has also two objections which would not, I think, occur to anyone nowadays. They stem from his neo-classical position. The first is that the behaviour of Iago and Othello is untrue to life because it is not 'soldierly'. The second is that the play has no moral.

Let us take these in order. The Renaissance derived most of its critical theory from Aristotle's *Poetics*, and there (1451 b 1) it found the doctrine of generality. 'The difference between the poet and the historian,' Aristotle tells us, 'does not lie in the fact that they express themselves in verse or prose . . . but in the fact that the historian speaks of what has happened, the poet of the kind of thing that *can* happen.' Some Renaissance critics took over this idea in the clumsy and restrictive form that all soldiers in literature must be soldierly, all kings must be kingly, all women womanly, all senators wise. Hence, to Rymer, Iago is 'a close, dissembling, false, insinuating rascal, instead of an open-hearted, frank, plain-dealing Souldier, a character constantly worn by them for some thousands of years in the World'. Next, the moral. Rymer wants the Aristotelian quadrivium of 'Plot, Character, Thought and Expression'; he thinks that a lofty play should give the audience some nugget of general wisdom to take home and examine, and the story of Othello seems too idiosyncratic for this. 'What,' he demands, 'can remain with the Audience to carry home with them from this sort of Poetry, for their use and edification?' and concludes satirically that it boils down to 'a warning to good housewives to look well to their linen'.

Both these objections were answered with characteristic firmness by Dr Johnson. In the great essay which forms the Preface to his edition of Shakespeare (1765), Johnson took pains to vindicate Shakespeare's truth to 'nature' against the narrow conception of 'nature' urged by such English writers as Rymer and John Dennis in his *An Essay on the Genius and Writings of Shakespeare* (1712), as also by Voltaire in *L'Appel à toutes les nations d'Europe* (1761):

> Dennis and Rymer think his Romans not sufficiently Roman; and Voltaire censures his kings as not completely royal. Dennis is offended that Menenius, a senator of Rome, should play the buffoon; and Voltaire perhaps thinks decency violated when the Danish usurper is represented as a drunkard. But Shakespeare always makes nature predominate over accident; and, if he preserves the essential character, is not very careful of distinctions superinduced and adventitious. His story requires Romans or kings, but he thinks only on men. He knew that Rome, like every other city, had men of all dispositions; and wanting a buffoon, he went into the senate house for that which the senate house would certainly have afforded him. He was inclined to show an usurper and a murderer not only odious, but despicable; he therefore added drunkenness to his other qualities, knowing that kings love wine like other men, and that wine exerts its natural power upon kings. These are the petty cavils of petty minds; a poet overlooks the casual distinction of country and condition, as a painter, satisfied with the figure, neglects the drapery.

As for Rymer's objection that *Othello* has no 'moral', teaches no wisdom, there will probably always be critics who will agree with him. (Wilson Knight's preliminary admission that *Othello* is 'a story of intrigue rather than a visionary statement' is, in its restated way, Rymerian.) But here again, Johnson was in no doubt, as we see from Boswell's account of their conversation (*Life*, 12 April 1776):

> I observed the great defect of the tragedy of *Othello* was that it had not a moral; for that no man could resist the circumstances of suspicion which were artfully suggested to Othello's mind.
>
> JOHNSON. 'In the first place, Sir, we learn from *Othello* this very useful moral, not to make an unequal match; in the second place, we learn not to yield too readily to suspicion. The handkerchief is merely a trick, though a very pretty trick; but there are no other circumstances of reasonable suspicion, except what is related by Iago of Cassio's warm expressions concerning Desdemona in his sleep; and that depended entirely upon the assertion of one man. No, Sir, I think *Othello* has more moral than almost any play.'

Johnson's line-by-line comments on the play, in his edition, show his usual perspicuity and humanity. They have, unfortunately, been crowded out of this overcrammed volume, but should be consulted either in Walter Raleigh's selection (*Johnson on Shakespeare*, 1908) or W. K. Wimsatt's *Samuel Johnson on Shakespeare* (New York, 1960), or, better still because complete, in the Yale edition of Johnson's *Works*. Neither Raleigh nor Wimsatt gives, for instance, the delicious note on 'I have rubb'd this young quat almost to the sense', nor the magisterial explication of:

> Patience, thou young and rose-lipp'd cheribin
> Ay, here, look grim as hell.

But Raleigh does at least give us Johnson's heartfelt note on Act v scene vi: 'I am glad that I have ended my revisal of this dreadful scene. It is not to be endured.'

VIII

All in all, *Othello* has provoked so much good critical writing that I have found the problem of space an insoluble one. In particular, the reader will find here no sustained discussion of Shakespeare's handling of his source, the unvarnished story of garrison intrigue and murder given in Giraldi Cinthio's *Hecatommithi* (1565); Kenneth Muir's masterly short treatment in his *Shakespeare's Sources* (vol. I, 1957, pp. 122–40) will provide the essential information, but the relationship of this play to its source is one of the most interesting in all Shakespeare's work, and should be borne in mind continually. Again, there is no discussion here of the text and its problems. The Cambridge 'New Shakespeare' volume, edited by Alice Walker and J. Dover Wilson (1957), provides an authoritative discussion of the matter, but the interested reader should follow also Nevill Coghill's argument in *Shakespeare's Professional Skills* (a book we have already pillaged twice), for Mr Coghill brings the experience of years of theatrical production to support his contention that the 1622 Quarto gives us the play as performed, and the 1623 Folio represents Shakespeare's own revisions after seeing how it worked out in performance.

A sense of the theatre will always be an asset in our effort to understand Shakespeare, and for that reason I should have liked, also, to include some of the interesting *dramatic* criticism that has survived, in which the critic not only reveals his attitude to the play but gives the flavour of some fine actor's performance, as Lamb recalled the Iago of Roland Bensley,[17] or Hazlitt conveyed the excitement of Kean's Othello,[18] or as, in our own time, John Russell Brown coolly anatomized the heady, voodoo magic of Olivier's Moor.[19] But, once again, space ran out. This play has called out the best in so many critics and actors, it has moved to their depths so many ordinary, inarticulate people who have left no record of their opinion, as to convince us once again that the response of humanity to a great work of art is almost as interesting as the work itself.

John Wain

NOTES

1. Louis Auchincloss, *Motiveless Malignity* (Boston, 1969) p. 7.
2. John Middleton Murry and, to some extent, R. B. Heilman.
3. David Kuala.
4. John E. Seaman, in *Shakespeare Quarterly*, XIX 81–5.
5. E. E. Stoll, *Othello, an historical and comparative study* (1915) and later works.
6. Heilman.
7. Emrys Jones.
8. Lilian Winstanley, *'Othello' as the Tragedy of Italy* (1924).
9. Macaulay, *Essay on Dante* (1824).
10. Rymer, *A Short View of Tragedy* (1693).
11. *Magic in the Web*, p. 166.
12. Cf. G. I. Duthie, *Shakespeare* (1951), p. 165: 'The tragedy in *Othello* is caused by two forces working in conjunction: it is caused by an external force of evil deliberately bringing itself to bear on a noble figure which has within it a *seed* of evil.'
13. Critical works referred to in section IV: J. A. Heraud, *Shakespeare, his Inner Life* (1865); D. J. Snider, *System of Shakespeare's Dramas* (1877); John W. Draper, 'Honest Iago', *PMLA* XLVI (1931); Mario Praz, 'Machiavelli and the Elizabethans', *Proceedings of the British Academy*, XIV (1928); William Hazlitt, *Characters of Shakespeare's Plays* (1817); Kenneth Muir, 'The Jealousy of Iago', *English Miscellany*, 2

(Rome, 1951). The views of the Exeter gentleman are summarized in the variorum *Othello*, ed. Furness (1886) pp. 408–9.

14. *Notes, criticism and correspondence upon Shakespeare's Plays and Actors* (New York, 1863).

15. For an illuminating discussion of Rymer's critical position, see Marvin T. Herrick, *The Poetics of Aristotle in England* (Yale and Oxford, 1930) pp. 57–62.

16. *The Influence of the Audience: Considerations Preliminary to the Psychological Analysis of Shakespeare's Characters* (New York, 1926).

17. 'On Some of the Old Actors', in *Elia* (1823).

18. *The Times*, 27 Oct 1817.

19. *Shakespeare Survey*, 18 (1965).

PART ONE

Earlier Comments

Thomas Rymer

FROM *A SHORT VIEW OF TRAGEDY* (1693)

ACT IV

Enter Jago *and* Othello.

Jago. *Will you think so?*
Othel. *Think so,* Jago!
Jago. *What, to kiss in private?*
Othel. *An unauthorised kiss.*
Jago. *Or to be naked with her friend a-bed*
An hour or more, not meaning any harm?
Othel. *Naked a-bed,* Jago, *and not mean harm!* –

At this gross rate of trifling, our General and his Auncient March on most heroically, till the Jealous Booby has his Brains turn'd, and falls in a Trance. Would any imagine this to be the Language of Venetians, of Souldiers and mighty Captains? no *Bartholomew* Droll cou'd subsist upon such trash. But lo, a Stratagem never presented in Tragedy:

Jago. *Stand you (a) while a part –*
—Incave your self,
And mark the Jeers, the Gibes, and notable scorns,
That dwell in every region of his face;
For I will make him tell the tale a new,
Where, how, how oft, how long ago, and when
He has and is again to Cope your Wife:
I say, but mark his gesture. –

With this device *Othello* withdraws. Says *Jago* aside:

Jago. *Now will I question* Cassio *of* Bianca,
A Huswife –
That doats on Cassio. –
He, when he hears of her, cannot refrain
From the excess of Laughter. –
As he shall smile, Othello *shall go mad;*
And his unbookish jealousy must conster
Poor Cassio's *smiles, gesture, and light behaviour,*
Quite in the wrong. –

So to work they go: And *Othello* is as wise a commentator, and makes his applications pat, as heart cou'd wish – but I wou'd not expect to find this Scene acted nearer than in *Southwark* Fair! But the *Handkerchief* is brought in at last, to stop all holes and close the evidence. So now being satisfied with the proof, they come to a resolution that the offenders shall be murdered.

Othel. – *But yet the pity of it,* Jago! *ah, the pity!*
Jago. *If you be so fond over her iniquity, give her Patent to offend. For if it touches not you, it comes near no Body.* –
Do it not with poison, strangle her in her Bed; Even the Bed she has contaminated.
Oth. *Good, good; the Justice of it pleases; very good.*
Jago. *And for* Cassio, *let me be his undertaker.* –

Jago had some pretence to be discontent with *Othello* and *Cassio*: And what passed hitherto was the operation of revenge. *Desdemona* had never done him harm, always kind to him and to his Wife, was his Country-woman, a Dame of quality: for him to abet her Murder shews nothing of a Souldier, nothing of a Man, nothing of Nature in it. The *Ordinary* of *Newgate* never had the like Monster to pass under his examination. Can it be any diversion to see a Rogue beyond what the Devil ever finish'd? Or wou'd it be any instruction to an Audience? *Jago* cou'd desire no better than to set *Cassio* and *Othello,* his two Enemies, by the Ears together, so he might have been reveng'd on them both at once: And chusing for his own share the Murder of *Desdemona*, he had the opportunity to play booty, and save the poor harmless wretch. But the Poet must do every thing by contraries, to surprize the Audience still with something horrible and prodigious beyond any human imagination. At this rate he must out-do the Devil to be a Poet in the rank with *Shakespear*.

Soon after this, arrives from *Venice Ludovico*, a noble Cousin of *Desdemona*; presently she is at him also on the behalf of *Cassio*.

Desd. *Cousin, there's fallen between him and my Lord*
An unkind breach; but you shall make all well.
Lud. *Is there division 'twixt my Lord and* Cassio?
Desd. *A most unhappy one; I would do much*
To attone them, for the love I bear to Cassio.

By this time we are to believe the couple have been a week or two Married: And *Othello*'s Jealousie, that had rag'd so loudly and had been so uneasie to himself, must have reach'd her knowledge. The *Audience* have all heard him more plain with her than was needful to a Venetian capacity: And yet she must still be impertinent in her suit for *Cassio*. Well, this *Magnifico* comes from the *Doge* and Senators to displace *Othello*.

Lud. – *Deputing* Cassio *in his Government.*
Desd. *Trust me, I am glad on't.*
Oth. *Indeed!*
Desd. *My Lord!*
Oth. *I am glad to see you mad.*
Desd. *How sweet* Othello?
Oth. *Devil!*
Desd. *I have not deserved this.*
Oth. *O Devil, Devil! –*
Out of my sight!
Desd. *I will not stay to offend you.*

Lud. *Truly, an obedient Lady.*
I do beseech your Lordship call her back.
Oth. *Mistress!*
Desd. *My Lord?*
Oth. *What would you with her, Sir?*
Lud. *Who, I, my Lord?*
Oth. *I, you did wish that I wou'd make her turn:*
Sir, she can turn, and turn, and yet go on,
And turn agen; and she can weep, Sir, weep;
And she is obedient, as you say, obedient,
Very obedient. –
Lud. *What, strike your Wife!*

Of what flesh and blood does our Poet make these noble Venetians, – the men without Gall, the Women without either Brain or Sense? A Senators Daughter runs away with this Black-amoor; the Government employs this Moor to defend them against the Turks, so resent not the Moors Marriage at present; but the danger over, her Father gets the Moor Cashier'd, sends his Kinsman, Seignior *Ludovico,* to *Cyprus* with the Commission for a new General; who, at his arrival, finds the Moor calling the Lady, his Kinswoman, Whore and Strumpet, and kicking her: what says the *Magnifico?*

Lud. *My Lord, this would not be believ'd in* Venice,
Tho' I shou'd swear I saw't; 'tis very much;
Make her amends: she weeps.

The Moor has no body to take his part, no body of his Colour; *Ludovico* has the new Governor, *Cassio,* and all his Countrymen Venetians about him. What Poet wou'd give a villanous Black-amoor this Ascendant? What Tramontain could fancy the Venetians so low, so despicable, or so patient? this outrage to an injur'd Lady, the *Divine Desdemona,* might in a colder Climate have provoked some body to be her Champion; but the Italians may well conclude we have a strange Genius for Poetry. In the next Scene *Othello* is examining the supposed Bawd; then follows another storm of horrour and outrage against the poor Chicken, his Wife. Some Drayman or drunken Tinker might possibly treat his drab at this sort of rate and mean no harm by it; but for his excellency, a My lord General, to Serenade a Senator's Daughter with such a volly of scoundrel filthy Language is sure the most absurd Maggot that ever bred from any Poets addle Brain.

And she is in the right, who tells us,

Emil. – *A Begger in his Drink*
Cou'd not have laid such terms upon his Callet.

This is not to describe passion. *Seneca* had another notion in the Case:

Parvae loquuntur curae, ingentes stupent.

And so had the Painter who drew *Agamemnon* with his Face covered. Yet to make all worse, her Murder, and the manner of it, had before been resolv'd upon and concerted. But nothing is to provoke a Venetian; she takes all in good part; had the Scene lain in *Russia,* what cou'd we have expected more? With us a Tinkers Trull wou'd be Nettled, wou'd repartee with more spirit, and not appear so void of spleen:

Desd. *O good* Jago,
What shall I do to win my Lord agen?

No woman bred out of a Pig-stye cou'd talk so meanly. After this she is call'd to Supper with *Othello, Ludovico,* &c.; after that comes a filthy sort of Pastoral Scene, where the *Wedding Sheets,* and Song of *Willow,* and her Mothers Maid, poor *Barbara,* are not the least moving things in this entertainment. But that we may not be kept too long in the dumps, nor the melancholy Scenes lye too heavy undigested on our Stomach, this *Act* gives us for a farewell the *salsa, O picante,* some quibbles and smart touches, as *Ovid* had Prophecied:

Est & in obscoenos deflexa Tragoedia risus.

The last *Act* begins with *Jago* and *Roderigo*: Who a little before had been upon the huff:

> Rod. *I say it is not very well. I will make my self known to* Desdemona*: if she will return me my Jewels, I will give over my suit and repent my unlawful sollicitation; if not, assure your self I'll seek satisfaction of you.*

Roderigo, a Noble Venetian, had sought *Desdemona* in Marriage, is troubled to find the Moor had got her from him, advises with *Jago,* who wheadles him to sell his Estate and go over the Sea to *Cyprus* in expectation to Cuckold *Othello*; there having cheated *Roderigo* of all his Money and Jewels on pretence of presenting them to *Desdemona,* our Gallant grows angry, and would have satisfaction from *Jago,* who sets all right by telling him *Cassio* is to be Governour, *Othello* is going with *Desdemona* into *Mauritania*; to prevent this, you are to murder *Cassio,* and then all may be well.

> Jago. *He goes into* Mauritania, *and takes with him the fair* Desdemona, *unless his abode be lingred here by some accident, wherein none can be so determinate as the removing of* Cassio.

Had *Roderigo* been one of the *Banditi,* he might not much stick at the Murder. But why *Roderigo* should take this for payment, and risque his person where the prospect of advantage is so very uncertain and remote, no body can imagine. It had need be a *super-subtle* Venetian that this Plot will pass upon. Then, after a little spurt of villany and Murder, we are brought to the most lamentable that ever appear'd on any Stage. A noble Venetian Lady is to be murdered by our Poet, – in sober sadness, purely for being a Fool. No Pagan Poet but wou'd have found some *Machine* for her deliverance. *Pegasus* wou'd have strain'd hard to have brought old *Perseus* on his back, time enough to rescue this *Andromeda* from so foul a Monster. Has our Christian Poetry no generosity, nor bowels? Ha, Sir *Lancelot*! ha, St *George*! will no Ghost leave the shades for us in extremity to save a distressed Damosel?

But for our comfort, however felonious is the Heart, hear with what soft language he does approach her, with a Candle in his Hand:

Oth. *Put out the light, and then put out the light:*
If I quench thee, thou flaming Minister,
I can again thy former light restore. –

Who would call him Barbarian, Monster, Savage? Is this a Black-amoor?

Soles occidere & redire possunt –

The very Soul and Quintessence of Sir *George Etheridge*!

One might think the General should not glory much in this action, but make an hasty work on't, and have turn'd his Eyes away from so unsouldierly an Execution; yet is he all pause and deliberation, handles her as calmly and is as careful of her Souls health as it had been her *Father Confessor. Have you prayed to Night,* Desdemona? But the suspence is necessary that he might have a convenient while so to *roul his Eyes,* and so to *gnaw* his *nether lip* to the spectators. Besides the greater cruelty – *sub tam lentis maxillis.*

But hark, a most tragical thing laid to her charge!

Oth. *That Handkerchief, that I so lov'd and gave thee,*
Thou gav'st to Cassio.
Desd. *No, by my Life and Soul!*
Send for the man, and ask him.
Oth. *By Heaven, I saw my Hankerchief in his hand.* –
– *I saw the Handkerchief.*

So much ado, so much stress, so much passion and repetition about an Handkerchief! Why was not this call'd the *Tragedy of the Handkerchief*? What can be more absurd than (as *Quintilian* expresses it) *in parvis litibus has Tragoedias movere*? We have heard of *Fortunatus his Purse* and of the *Invisible Cloak,* long ago worn threadbare and stow'd up in the Wardrobe of obsolete Romances: one might think that were a fitter place for this Handkerchief than that it, at this time of day, be worn on the Stage, to raise every where all this clutter and turmoil. Had it been *Desdemona*'s Garter, the Sagacious Moor might have smelt a Rat; but the Handkerchief is so remote a trifle, no Booby on this side *Mauritania* cou'd make any consequence from it.

We may learn here that a Woman never loses her Tongue, even tho' after she is stifl'd:

Desd. *O falsly, falsly murder'd!*
Em. *Sweet* Desdemona, *O sweet Mistress, speak!*
Desd. *A guiltless death I dye.*
Em. *O who has done the deed?*
Desd. *No body; I my self; farewel:*
Commend me to my kind Lord; O farewel!

This *Desdemona* is a black swan, or an old Blackamoor is a bewitching Bed-fellow. If this be Nature, it is a *lascheté* below what the English Language can express.

For *Lardella* to *make love like an Humble Bee* was, in *The Rehearsal,* thought a fancy odd enough.

But hark what follows:

Oth. – *O heavy hour!*
Methinks it shou'd be now a huge Eclipse
Of Sun and Moon, and that the affrighted globe
Shou'd yawn at Alteration.

This is wonderful! Here is Poetry to *elevate* and *amuse*. Here is sound All-sufficient. It wou'd be uncivil to ask *Flamstead* if the Sun and Moon can both together be so hugely eclipsed in any *heavy hour* whatsoever. Nor must the Spectators consult *Gresham* Colledge whether a body is naturally *frighted* till he *Yawn* agen. The Fortune of *Greece* is not concern'd with these Matters. These are Physical circumstances a Poet may be ignorant in, without any harm to the publick. These slips have no influence on our Manners and good Life, which are the Poets Province.

Rather may we ask here what unnatural crime *Desdemona* or her Parents had committed, to bring this Judgment down upon her: to Wed a Black-amoor, and innocent to be thus cruelly murder'd by him. What instruction can we make out of this Catastrophe? Or whither must our reflection lead us? Is not this to envenome and sour our spirits, to make us repine and grumble at Providence and the government of the World? If this be our end, what boots it to be Vertuous?

Desdemona dropt the Handkerchief, and missed it that very day after her Marriage; it might have been rumpl'd up with her Wedding sheets: And this Night that she lay in her wedding sheets, the *Fairey* Napkin (whilst *Othello* was stifling her) might have started up to disarm his fury and stop his ungracious mouth. Then might she (in a Traunce for fear) have lain as dead. Then might he, believing her dead, touch'd with remorse, have honestly cut his own Throat, by the good leave and with the applause of all the Spectators: Who might thereupon have gone home with a quiet mind, admiring the beauty of Providence, fairly and truly represented on the Theatre.

Oth. – *Why, how shou'd she be murdered?*
Em. *Alas, who knows?*
Oth. *You heard her say her self, it was not I.*
Em. *She did so; I must needs report a truth.*
Oth. *She's like a liar gone to burn in Hell.*
'Twas I that did it.
Em. *O, the more Angel she,*

And you the blacker Devil!
Oth. *She turn'd to folly, and she was an Whore.*
Em. *Thou dost belye her, and thou art a Devil.*
Oth. *She was false as Water.*
Em. *Thou art rash as Fire,*
To say that she was false: O, she was heavenly true.

In this kind of Dialogue they continue for forty lines farther, before she bethinks her self to cry Murder.

Em. – *Help, help, O help!*
The Moor has kill'd my Mistress! murder, murder!

But from this Scene to the end of the Play we meet with nothing but blood and butchery, described much-what to the style of *the last Speeches and Confessions of the persons executed at Tyburn*; with this difference, that there we have the *fact* and the due course of Justice, whereas our Poet, against all Justice and Reason, against all Law, Humanity, and Nature, in a barbarous, arbitrary way, executes and makes havock of his subjects, *Hab-nab,* as they come to hand. *Desdemona* dropt her Handkerchief; therefore she must be stifl'd. *Othello,* by law to be broken on the Wheel, by the Poets cunning escapes with cutting his own Throat. *Cassio,* for I know not what, comes off with a broken shin. *Jago* murders his Benefactor *Roderigo,* as this were poetical gratitude. *Jago* is not yet kill'd, because there yet never was such a villain alive. The Devil, if once he brings a man to be dipt in a deadly sin, lets him alone to take his course; and now when the *Foul Fiend* has done with him, our wise Authors take the sinner into their poetical service, there to accomplish him and do the Devils drudgery.

Philosophy tells us it is a principle in the Nature of Man *to be grateful.*

History may tell us that *John an Oaks, John a Stiles,* or *Jago* were ungrateful. *Poetry* is to follow Nature; Philosophy must be his guide: history and *fact* in particular cases of *John an Oaks* or *John of Styles* are no warrant or direction for a Poet. Therefore *Aristotle* is always telling us that Poetry is σπουδαιότερον καὶ φιλοσοφώτερον, is more general and abstracted, is led more by the Philosophy, the reason and nature of things than History, which only records things higlety piglety, right or wrong, as they happen. History might without any preamble or difficulty say that *Jago* was ungrateful. Philosophy then calls him unnatural. But the Poet is not without huge labour and preparation to expose the Monster, and after shew the Divine Vengeance executed upon him. The Poet is not to add wilful Murder to his ingratitude: he has not antidote enough for the Poison: his Hell and Furies are not punishment sufficient for one single crime of that bulk and aggravation.

Em. *O thou dull Moor, that Handkerchief thou speakest on*
I found by Fortune and did give my Husband;
For often with a solemn earnestness,
More than indeed belong'd to such a trifle,
He beg'd of me to steal it.

Here we see the meanest woman in the Play takes this *Handkerchief* for a *trifle* below her Husband to trouble his head about it. Yet we find it entered into our Poets head to make a Tragedy of this *Trifle.*

Then, for the *unraveling of the Plot,* as they call it, never was old deputy Recorder in a Country Town, with his spectacles, in summoning up the evidence, at such a puzzle, so blunder'd and be-doultefied, as is our Poet to have a good riddance, And get the *Catastrophe* off his hands.

What can remain with the Audience to carry home with them from this sort of Poetry for their use and edification? how can it work, unless (instead of settling the mind and purging our passions) to delude our senses, disorder our thoughts, addle our brain, pervert our affections, hair our imaginations, corrupt our appetite, and fill our head with vanity, confusion, *Tin-*

tamarre, and Jingle-jangle, beyond what all the Parish Clarks of *London* with their *old Testament* farces and interludes, in *Richard* the seconds time, cou'd ever pretend to? Our only hopes for the good of their Souls can be that these people go to the Playhouse as they do to Church, to sit still, look on one another, make no reflection, nor mind the Play more than they would a Sermon.

There is in this Play some burlesk, some humour and ramble of Comical Wit, some shew and some *Mimickry* to divert the spectators; but the tragical part is plainly none other than a Bloody Farce, without salt or savour.

Samuel Johnson

GENERAL REMARKS ON *OTHELLO* (1765)

The beauties of this play impress themselves so strongly upon the attention of the reader, that they can draw no aid from critical illustration. The fiery openness of *Othello*, magnanimous, artless, and credulous, boundless in his confidence, ardent in his affection, inflexible in his resolution, and obdurate in his revenge; the cool malignity of *Iago*, silent in his resentment, subtle in his designs, and studious at once of his interest and his vengeance; the soft simplicity of *Desdemona*, confident of merit, and conscious of innocence, her artless perseverance in her suit, and her slowness to suspect that she can be suspected, are such proofs of *Shakespeare*'s skill in human nature, as, I suppose, it is vain to seek in any modern writer. The gradual progress which *Iago* makes in the Moor's conviction, and the circumstances which he employs to inflame him, are so artfully natural, that, though it will perhaps not be said of him as he says of himself, that he is *a man not easily jealous*, yet we cannot but pity him when at last we find him *perplexed in the extreme*.

There is always danger lest wickedness conjoined with abilities should steal upon esteem, though it misses of approbation; but the character of *Iago* is so conducted, that he is from the first scene to the last hated and despised.

Even the inferiour characters of this play would be very conspicuous in any other piece, not only for their justness but their strength. *Cassio* is brave, benevolent, and honest, ruined only by his want of stubbornness to resist an insidious invitation. *Roderigo*'s suspicious credulity, and impatient submission to the cheats which he sees practised upon him, and which by persuasion he suffers to be repeated, exhibit a strong picture of a weak mind betrayed by unlawful desires, to a false friend; and the virtue of *Aemilia* is such as we often find, worn loosely, but not cast off, easy to commit small crimes, but quickened and alarmed at atrocious villanies.

The Scenes from the beginning to the end are busy, varied by happy interchanges, and regularly promoting the progression of the story; and the narrative in the end, though it tells but what is known already, yet is necessary to produce the death of *Othello*.

Had the scene opened in *Cyprus*, and the preceding incidents been occasionally related, there had been little wanting to a drama of the most exact and scrupulous regularity.

SOURCE: Johnson's *Shakespeare* (1765).

S. T. Coleridge

MARGINALIA ON *OTHELLO*

[I iii 292–4.

Bra. Look to her, Moor, if thou hast eyes to see:
She has deceived her father, and may thee.
Oth. My life upon her faith!]

In real life how do we look back to little speeches, either as presentimental [of], or most contrasted with, an affecting event. Shakespeare, as secure of being read over and over, of becoming a family friend, how he provides this for *his readers,* and leaves it to them.

[I iii 319–20.

Iago. Virtue! a fig! 'tis in ourselves that we are thus or thus.]

Iago's passionless character, all *will* in intellect; therefore a bold partizan here of a truth, but yet of a truth converted into falsehood by absence of all the modifications by the frail nature of man. And the *last sentiment* –

[... our raging motions, our carnal stings, our unbitted lusts; whereof I take this, that you call love, to be a sect or scion] –

There lies the Iagoism of how many! And the repetition, 'Go make money!' – a pride in it, of an anticipated dupe, stronger than the love of lucre.

[I iii 377–8. First Quarto and Stockdale text:

Iago. Go to, farewell, put money enough in your purse:
Thus do I ever make my fool my purse.]

The triumph! Again, 'put money,' after the effect has been fully produced. The last speech, [Iago's soliloquy,] the motive-hunting of motiveless malignity – how awful! In itself fiendish; while yet he was allowed to bear the divine image, too fiendish for his own steady view. A being next to devil, only *not* quite devil – and this Shakespeare has attempted – executed – without disgust, without scandal!

REPORT OF A LECTURE AT BRISTOL (November 1813)

[LECTURE IV]

[*Winter's Tale, Othello*]

At the commencement of the fourth lecture last evening, Mr Coleridge combated the opinion held by some critics, that the writings of Shakespeare were like a wilderness, in which were desolate places, most beautiful flowers, and weeds; he argued that even the titles of his plays were appropriate and shewed judgment, presenting as it were a bill of fare before the feast. This was peculiarly so in *The Winter's Tale*, – a wild story, calculated to interest a circle round a fireside. He maintained that Shakespeare ought not to be judged of in detail, but on the whole. A pedant differed from a master in cramping himself with certain established rules, whereas the master regarded rules as always controllable by and subservient to the end. The passion to be delineated in *The Winter's Tale* was *jealousy*. Shakespeare's description of this, however, was perfectly philosophical: the mind, in its first harbouring of it, became mean and despicable, and the first sensation was perfect shame, arising from the consideration of having possessed an object unworthily, of degrading a person to a thing. The mind that once indulges this passion has a predisposition, a vicious weakness, by which it kindles a fire from every spark, and from circumstances the most innocent and indifferent finds fuel to feed the flame. This he exemplified in an able manner from the conduct and opinion of Leontes, who seized upon occurrences of which he himself was the cause, and when speaking of Hermione, combined his anger with images of the lowest sensuality, and pursued the object with the utmost cruelty. This character Mr Coleridge contrasted with that of Othello, whom Shakespeare had portrayed the very opposite to a jealous man: he was noble, generous, open-hearted; unsuspicious and unsuspecting; and who, even after the exhibition of the handkerchief as evidence of his wife's guilt, bursts out in her praise. Mr C. ridiculed the idea of making Othello a negro. He was a gallant Moor, of royal blood, combining a high sense of Spanish and Italian feeling, and whose noble nature was wrought on, not by a fellow with a countenance predestined for the gallows, as some actors represented Iago, but by an accomplished and artful villain, who was indefatigable in his exertions to poison the mind of the brave and swarthy Moor. It is impossible, with our limits, to follow Mr Coleridge through those nice discriminations by which he elucidated the various characters in this excellent drama. Speaking of the character of the women of Shakespeare, or rather, as Pope stated, the absence of character, Mr Coleridge said this was the highest compliment that could be paid to them: the elements were so commixed, so even was the balance of feeling, that no one protruded in particular, – everything amiable as sisters, mothers, and wives, was included in the thought. To form a just estimation and to enjoy the beauties of Shakespeare, Mr Coleridge's lectures should be *heard* again and again. Perhaps at some future period we may occasionally fill our columns with an analysis of his different lectures similar to what we presented last week of the first; at present we must content ourselves with generals.

SOURCE: *Shakespearean Criticism* (ed. T. M. Raysor; 2nd edition, 1960).

PART TWO

Recent Studies

A. C. Bradley

FROM *SHAKESPEAREAN TRAGEDY* (1904)*

... Othello is, in one sense of the word, by far the most romantic figure among Shakespeare's heroes; and he is so partly from the strange life of war and adventure which he has lived from childhood. He does not belong to our world, and he seems to enter it we know not whence – almost as if from wonderland. There is something mysterious in his descent from men of royal siege; in his wanderings in vast deserts and among marvellous peoples; in his tales of magic handkerchiefs and prophetic Sibyls; in the sudden vague glimpses we get of numberless battles and sieges in which he has played the hero and has borne a charmed life; even in chance references to his baptism, his being sold to slavery, his sojourn in Aleppo.

And he is not merely a romantic figure; his own nature is romantic. He has not, indeed, the meditative or speculative imagination of Hamlet; but in the strictest sense of the word he is more poetic than Hamlet. Indeed, if one recalls Othello's most famous speeches – those that begin, 'Her father loved me', 'O now for ever', 'Never, Iago', 'Had it pleased Heaven', 'It is the cause', 'Behold, I have a weapon', 'Soft you, a word or two before you go' – and if one places side by side with these speeches an equal number by any other hero, one will not doubt that Othello is the greatest poet of them all. There is the same poetry in his casual phrases – like 'These nine moons wasted',

* [*Editor's note.*] The fragment here reprinted is not intended to represent Bradley's detailed and subtle essay in anything like its full range, but it should illustrate his attitude and method. The full text is easily available.

'Keep up your bright swords, for the dew will rust them', 'You chaste stars', 'It is a sword of Spain, the ice-brook's temper', 'It is the very error of the moon' – and in those brief expressions of intense feeling which ever since have been taken as the absolute expression, like

> If it were now to die,
> 'Twere now to be most happy; for, I fear,
> My soul hath her content so absolute
> That not another comfort like to this
> Succeeds in unknown fate,

or

> If she be false, O then Heaven mocks itself,
> I'll not believe it;

or

> No, my heart is turned to stone; I strike it, and it hurts my hand,

or

> But yet the pity of it, Iago! O Iago, the pity of it, Iago!

or

> O thou weed,
> Who are so lovely fair and smell'st so sweet
> That the sense aches at thee, would thou hadst ne'er been born.

And this imagination, we feel, has accompanied his whole life. He has watched with a poet's eye the Arabian trees dropping their med'cinable gum, and the Indian throwing away his chance-found pearl; and has gazed in a fascinated dream at the Pontic sea rushing, never to return, to the Propontic and the Hellespont;

and has felt as no other man ever felt (for he speaks of it as none other ever did) the poetry of the pride, pomp, and circumstance of glorious war.

So he comes before us, dark and grand, with a light upon him from the sun where he was born; but no longer young, and now grave, self-controlled, steeled by the experience of countless perils, hardships and vicissitudes, at once simple and stately in bearing and in speech, a great man naturally modest but fully conscious of his worth, proud of his services to the state, unawed by dignitaries and unelated by honours, secure, it would seem, against all dangers from without and all rebellion from within. And he comes to have his life crowned with the final glory of love, a love as strange, adventurous and romantic as any passage of his eventful history, filling his heart with tenderness and his imagination with ecstasy. For there is no love, not that of Romeo in his youth, more steeped in imagination than Othello's.

The sources of danger in this character are revealed but too clearly by the story. In the first place, Othello's mind, for all its poetry, is very simple. He is not observant. His nature tends outward. He is quite free from introspection, and is not given to reflection. Emotion excites his imagination, but it confuses and dulls his intellect. On this side he is the very opposite of Hamlet, with whom, however, he shares a great openness and trustfulness of nature. In addition, he has little experience of the corrupt products of civilised life, and is ignorant of European women.

In the second place, for all his dignity and massive calm (and he has greater dignity than any other of Shakespeare's men), he is by nature full of the most vehement passion. Shakespeare emphasises his self-control, not only by the wonderful pictures of the First Act, but by references to the past. Lodovico, amazed at his violence, exclaims:

> Is this the noble Moor whom our full Senate
> Call all in all sufficient? Is this the nature

Whom passion could not shake? whose solid virtue
The shot of accident nor dart of chance
Could neither graze nor pierce?

Iago, who has here no motive for lying, asks:

Can he be angry? I have seen the cannon
When it hath blown his ranks into the air,
And, like the devil, from his very arm
Puffed his own brother – and can he be angry?*

This, and other aspects of his character, are best exhibited by a single line – one of Shakespeare's miracles – the words by which Othello silences in a moment the night-brawl between his attendants and those of Brabantio:

Keep up your bright swords, for the dew will rust them.

And the same self-control is strikingly shown where Othello endeavours to elicit some explanation of the fight between Cassio and Montano. Here, however, there occur ominous words, which make us feel how necessary was this self-control, and make us admire it the more:

Now, by heaven,
My blood begins my safer guides to rule,
And passion, having my best judgment collied,
Assays to lead the way.

We remember these words later, when the sun of reason is 'collied', blackened and blotted out in total eclipse.

Lastly, Othello's nature is all of one piece. His trust, where he trusts, is absolute. Hesitation is almost impossible to him. He is extremely self-reliant, and decides

* For the actor, then, to represent him as violently angry when he cashiers Cassio is an utter mistake.

and acts instantaneously. If stirred to indignation, as 'in Aleppo once', he answers with one lightning stroke. Love, if he loves, must be to him the heaven where either he must live or bear no life. If such a passion as jealousy seizes him, it will swell into a well-nigh incontrollable flood. He will press for immediate conviction or immediate relief. Convinced, he will act with the authority of a judge and the swiftness of a man in mortal pain. Undeceived, he will do like execution on himself.

This character is so noble, Othello's feelings and actions follow so inevitably from it and from the forces brought to bear on it, and his sufferings are so heartrending, that he stirs, I believe, in most readers a passion of mingled love and pity which they feel for no other hero in Shakespeare, and to which not even Mr Swinburne can do more than justice. Yet there are some critics and not a few readers who cherish a grudge against him. They do not merely think that in the later stages of his temptation he showed a certain obtuseness, and that, to speak pedantically, he acted with unjustifiable precipitance and violence; no one, I suppose, denies that. But, even when they admit that he was not of a jealous temper, they consider that he *was* 'easily jealous'; they seem to think that it was inexcusable in him to feel any suspicion of his wife at all; and they blame him for never suspecting Iago or asking him for evidence. I refer to this attitude of mind chiefly in order to draw attention to certain points in the story. It comes partly from mere inattention (for Othello did suspect Iago and did ask him for evidence); partly from a misconstruction of the text which makes Othello appear jealous long before he really is so;* and partly from failure to realise certain essential facts. I will begin with these.

1. Othello, we have seen, was trustful, and thorough in his trust. He put entire confidence in the honesty of Iago, who had not only been his companion in arms,

* I cannot deal fully with this point in the lecture.

but, as he believed, had just proved his faithfulness in the matter of the marriage. This confidence was misplaced, and we happen to know it; but it was no sign of stupidity in Othello. For his opinion of Iago was the opinion of practically everyone who knew him: and that opinion was that Iago was before all things 'honest', his very faults being those of excess in honesty. This being so, even if Othello had not been trustful and simple, it would have been quite unnatural in him to be unmoved by the warnings of so honest a friend, warnings offered with extreme reluctance and manifestly from a sense of a friend's duty.* *Any* husband would have been troubled by them.

2. Iago does not bring these warnings to a husband who had lived with a wife for months and years and knew her like his sister or his bosom-friend. Nor is there any ground in Othello's character for supposing that, if he had been such a man, he would have felt and acted as he does in the play. But he was newly married; in the circumstances he cannot have known much of Desdemona before his marriage; and further he was conscious of being under the spell of a feeling which can give glory to the truth but can also give it to a dream.

3. This consciousness in any imaginative man is enough, in such circumstances, to destroy his confidence in his powers of perception. In Othello's case, after a long and most artful preparation, there now comes, to reinforce its effect, the suggestions that he is not an Italian, nor even a European; that he is totally ignorant of the thoughts and the customary morality of

* It is important to observe that, in his attempt to arrive at the facts about Cassio's drunken misdemeanour, Othello had just had an example of Iago's unwillingness to tell the whole truth where it must injure a friend. No wonder he feels in the Temptation-scene that 'this honest creature doubtless Sees and knows more, much more, than he unfolds'.

† To represent that Venetian women do not regard adultery so seriously as Othello does, and again that Othello would be wise to accept the situation like an Italian husband, is one of Iago's most artful and most maddening devices.

Venetian women; that he had himself seen in Desdemona's deception of her father how perfect an actress she could be. As he listens in horror, for a moment at least the past is revealed to him in a new and dreadful light, and the ground seems to sink under his feet. These suggestions are followed by a tentative but hideous and humiliating insinuation of what his honest and much-experienced friend fears may be the true explanation of Desdemona's rejection of acceptable suitors, and of her strange, and naturally temporary, preference for a black man. Here Iago goes too far. He sees something in Othello's face that frightens him, and he breaks off. Nor does this idea take any hold of Othello's mind. But it is not surprising that his utter powerlessness to repel it on the ground of knowledge of his wife, or even of that instinctive interpretation of character which is possible between persons of the same race,* should complete his misery, so that he feels he can bear no more, and abruptly dismisses his friend (III iii 238).

Now I repeat that *any* man situated as Othello was would have been disturbed by Iago's communications, and I add that many men would have been made wildly jealous. But up to this point, where Iago is dismissed, Othello, I must maintain, does not show jealousy. His confidence is shaken, he is confused and deeply troubled, he feels even horror; but he is not yet jealous in the proper sense of that word. In his soliloquy (III iii 258 ff.) the beginning of this passion may be traced; but it is only after an interval of solitude, when he has had time to dwell on the idea presented to him, and especially after statements of fact, not mere general

* If the reader has even chanced to see an African violently excited, he may have been startled to observe how completely at a loss he was to interpret those bodily expressions of passion which in a fellow-countryman he understands at once, and in a European foreigner with somewhat less certainty. The effect of difference in blood in increasing Othello's bewilderment regarding his wife is not sufficiently realised. The same effect has to be remembered in regard to Desdemona's mistakes in dealing with Othello in his anger.

grounds of suspicion, are offered, that the passion lays hold of him. Even then, however, and indeed to the very end, he is quite unlike the essentially jealous man, quite unlike Leontes. No doubt the thought of another man's possessing the woman he loves is intolerable to him; no doubt the sense of insult and the impulse of revenge are at times most violent; and these are the feelings of jealousy proper. But these are not the chief or the deepest source of Othello's suffering. It is the wreck of his faith and his love. It is the feeling,

> If she be false, oh then Heaven mocks itself;

the feeling,

> O Iago, the pity of it, Iago!

the feeling,

> But there where I have garner'd up my heart,
> Where either I must live, or bear no life;
> The fountain from the which my current runs,
> Or else dries up – to be discarded thence....

You will find nothing like this in Leontes.

Up to this point, it appears to me, there is not a syllable to be said against Othello. But the play is a tragedy, and from this point we may abandon the ungrateful and undramatic task of awarding praise and blame. When Othello, after a brief interval, re-enters (III iii 330), we see at once that the poison has been at work, and 'burns like the mines of sulphur'.

> Look where he comes! Not poppy, nor mandragora,
> Nor all the drowsy syrups of the world,
> Shall ever medicine thee to that sweet sleep
> Which thou owedst yesterday.

He is 'on the rack', in an agony so unbearable that he

cannot endure the sight of Iago. Anticipating the probability that Iago has spared him the whole truth, he feels that in that case his life is over and his 'occupation gone' with all its glories. But he has not abandoned hope. The bare possibility that his friend is deliberately deceiving him – though such a deception would be a thing so monstrously wicked that he can hardly conceive it credible – is a kind of hope. He furiously demands proof, ocular proof. And when he is compelled to see that he is demanding an impossibility he still demands evidence. He forces it from the unwilling witness, and hears the maddening tale of Cassio's dream. It is enough. And if it were not enough, has he not sometimes seen a handkerchief spotted with strawberries in his wife's hand? Yes, it was his first gift to her.

> I know not that; but such a handkerchief –
> I am sure it was your wife's – did I to-day
> See Cassio wipe his beard with.

'If it be that,' he answers – but what need to test the fact? The 'madness of revenge' is in his blood, and hesitation is a thing he never knew. He passes judgment, and controls himself only to make his sentence a solemn vow.

The Othello of the Fourth Act is Othello in his fall. His fall is never complete, but he is much changed. Towards the close of the Temptation-scene he becomes at times most terrible, but his grandeur remains almost undiminished. Even in the following scene (III iv), where he goes to test Desdemona in the matter of the handkerchief, and receives a fatal confirmation of her guilt, our sympathy with him is hardly touched by any feeling of humiliation. But in the Fourth Act 'Chaos has come'. A slight interval of time may be admitted here. It is but slight; for it was necessary for Iago to hurry on, and terribly dangerous to leave a chance for a meeting of Cassio with Othello; and his insight into Othello's nature taught him that his plan was to deliver blow on blow, and never to allow his victim to recover from the confusion of the first shock. Still there is a slight interval; and when Othello reappears we see at a glance that he is a changed man. He is physically exhausted, and his mind is dazed. He sees everything blurred through a mist of blood and tears. He has actually forgotten the incident of the handkerchief, and has to be reminded of it. When Iago, perceiving that he can now risk almost any lie, tells him that Cassio has confessed his guilt, Othello, the hero who has seemed to us only second to Coriolanus in physical power, trembles all over; he mutters disjointed words; a blackness suddenly intervenes between his eyes and the world; he takes it for the shuddering testimony of nature to the horror he has just heard,* and he falls senseless to the ground. When he recovers it is to watch Cassio, as he imagines, laughing over his shame. It is an imposition so gross, and should have been one so perilous, that Iago would never have ventured it before. But he is safe now. The sight only adds to the confusion of intellect the madness of rage; and a ravenous thirst for revenge, contending with motions of infinite longing and regret, conquers them. The delay till night-fall is torture to him. His self-control has wholly deserted him, and he strikes his wife in the presence of the Venetian envoy. He is so lost to all sense of reality that he never asks himself what will follow the deaths of Cassio and his wife. An ineradicable instinct of justice, rather than any last quiver of hope, leads him

* Cf. *Winter's Tale*, I ii 137 ff.:

Can thy dam? – may't be?–
Affection! thy intention stabs the centre:
Thou dost make possible things not so held,
Communicatest with dreams; – how can this be?
With what's unreal thou coactive art,
And fellow'st nothing: then 'tis very credent
Thou may'st cojoin with something; and thou dost,
And that beyond commission, and I find it,
And that to the infection of my brains
And hardening of my brows.

to question Emilia; but nothing could convince him now, and there follows the dreadful scene of accusation; and then, to allow us the relief of burning hatred and burning tears, this interview of Desdemona with Iago, and that last talk of hers with Emilia, and her last song.

But before the end there is again a change. The supposed death of Cassio (v i) satiates the thirst for vengeance. The Othello who enters the bed-chamber with the words,

> It is the cause, it is the cause, my soul,

is not the man of the Fourth Act. The deed he is bound to do is no murder, but a sacrifice. He is to save Desdemona from herself, not in hate but in honour; in honour, and also in love. His anger has passed; a boundless sorrow has taken its place; and

> this sorrow's heavenly:
> It strikes where it doth love.

Even when, at the sight of her apparent obduracy, and at the hearing of words which by a crowning fatality can only reconvince him of her guilt, these feelings give way to others, it is to righteous indignation they give way, not to rage; and, terribly painful as this scene is, there is almost nothing here to diminish the admiration and love which heighten pity. And pity itself vanishes, and love and admiration alone remain, in the majestic dignity and sovereign ascendancy of the close. Chaos has come and gone; and the Othello of the Council-chamber and the quay of Cyprus has returned, or a greater and nobler Othello still. As he speaks those final words in which all the glory and agony of his life – long ago in India and Arabia and Aleppo, and afterwards in Venice, and now in Cyprus – seem to pass before us, like the pictures that flash before the eyes of a drowning man, a triumphant scorn for the fetters of the flesh and the littleness of all the lives that must survive him sweeps our grief away, and when he dies upon a kiss the most painful of all tragedies leaves us for the moment free from pain, and exulting in the power of 'love and man's unconquerable mind'.

T. S. Eliot

FROM 'SHAKESPEARE AND THE STOICISM OF SENECA' (1927)

I want to be quite definite in my notion of the possible influence of Seneca on Shakespeare. I think it is quite likely that Shakespeare read some of Seneca's tragedies at school. I think it quite unlikely that Shakespeare knew anything of that extraordinarily dull and uninteresting body of Seneca's prose, which was translated by Lodge and printed in 1612. So far as Shakespeare was influenced by Seneca, it was by his memories of school conning and through the influence of the Senecan tragedy of the day, through Kyd and Peele, but chiefly Kyd. That Shakespeare deliberately took a 'view of life' from Seneca there seems to be no evidence whatever.

Nevertheless, there is, in some of the great tragedies of Shakespeare, a new attitude. It is not the attitude of Seneca, but is derived from Seneca; it is slightly different from anything that can be found in French tragedy, in Corneille or in Racine; it is modern, and it culminates, if there is ever any culmination, in the attitude of Nietzsche, I cannot say that it is Shakespeare's philosophy'. Yet many people have lived by it; though it may only have been Shakespeare's instinctive recognition of something of theatrical utility. It is the attitude of self-dramatization assumed by some of Shakespeare's heroes at moments of tragic intensity. It is not peculiar to Shakespeare; it is conspicuous in Chapman: Bussy, Clermont and Biron, all die in this way. Marston – one of the most interesting and least explored of all the Elizabethans – uses it; and Marston and Chapman were particularly Senecan. But Shakespeare, of course, does it very much better than any of the others, and makes it somehow more integral with the human nature of his characters. It is less verbal, more real. I have always felt that I have never read a more terrible exposure of human weakness – of universal human weakness – than the last great speech of Othello. (I am ignorant whether anyone else has ever adopted this view, and it may appear subjective and fantastic in the extreme.) It is usually taken on its face value, as expressing the greatness in defeat of a noble but erring nature.

Soft you; a word or two before you go.
I have done the state some service, and they know't.
No more of that. I pray you, in your letters,
When you shall these unlucky deeds relate,
Speak of me as I am; nothing extenuate,
Nor set down aught in malice: then must you speak
Of one that loved not wisely but too well;
Of one not easily jealous, but, being wrought,
Perplex'd in the extreme; of one whose hand,
Like the base Indian, threw a pearl away
Richer than all his tribe; of one whose subdued eyes,
Albeit unused to the melting mood,
Drop tears as fast as the Arabian trees
Their medicinal gum. Set you down this;
And say, besides, that in Aleppo once,
Where a malignant and a turban'd Turk
Beat a Venetian and traduced the state,
I took by the throat the circumcised dog,
And smote him, thus.

What Othello seems to me to be doing in making this speech is *cheering himself up*. He is endeavouring to escape reality, he has ceased to think about Desdemona, and is thinking about himself. Humility is the most difficult of all virtues to achieve; nothing dies harder than the desire to think well of oneself. Othello succeeds in turning himself into a pathetic figure, by adopting an *aesthetic* rather than a moral attitude, dramatizing himself against his environment. He takes in the spectator, but the human motive is primarily to take in himself. I do not believe that any writer has ever exposed this *bovarysme*, the human will to see things as they are not, more clearly than Shakespeare.

If you compare the deaths of several of Shakespeare's heroes – I do not say *all*, for there are very few generalizations that can be applied to the whole of Shakespeare's work – but notably Othello, Coriolanus and Antony – with the deaths of heroes of dramatists such as Marston and Chapman, consciously under Senecan influence, you will find a strong similarity – except only that Shakespeare does it both more poetically and more lifelike.

SOURCE: *Selected Essays* (1932)

G. Wilson Knight

THE *OTHELLO* MUSIC (1930)

In *Othello* we are faced with the vividly particular rather than the vague and universal. The play as a whole has a distinct formal beauty: within it we are ever confronted with beautiful and solid forms. The persons tend to appear as warmly human, concrete. They are neither vaguely universalized, as in *King Lear* or *Macbeth*, nor deliberately mechanized and vitalized by the poet's philosophic plan as in *Measure for Measure* and *Timon of Athens*, wherein the significance of the dramatic person is dependent almost wholly on our understanding of the allegorical or symbolical meaning. It is true that Iago is here a mysterious, inhuman creature of unlimited cynicism: but the very presence of the concrete creations around, in differentiating him sharply from the rest, limits and defines him. *Othello* is a story of intrigue rather than a visionary statement. If, however, we tend to regard Othello, Desdemona, and Iago as suggestive symbols rather than human beings, we may, from a level view of their interaction, find a clear relation existing between *Othello* and other plays of the hate-theme. Such an anaylsis will be here only in part satisfactory. It exposes certain underlying ideas, abstracts them from the original: it is less able to interpret the whole positive beauty of the play. With this important reservation, I shall push the interpretative method as far as possible.

Othello is dominated by its protagonist. Its supremely beautiful effects of style are all expressions of Othello's personal passion. Thus, in first analysing Othello's poetry, we shall lay the basis for an understanding of the play's symbolism: this matter of style is, indeed, crucial, and I shall now indicate those qualities which clearly distinguish it from other Shakespearian poetry. It holds a rich music all its own, and possesses a unique solidity and precision of picturesque phrase or image, a peculiar chastity and serenity of thought. It is, as a rule, barren of direct metaphysical content. Its thought does not mesh with the reader's: rather it is always outside us, aloof. This aloofness is the resultant of an inward aloofness of image from image, word from word. The dominant quality is separation, not, as is more usual in Shakespeare, cohesion. Consider these exquisite poetic movements:

O heavy hour!
Methinks it should be now a huge eclipse
Of sun and moon, and that the affrighted globe
Should yawn at alteration. (v ii 97)

Or,

It is the very error of the moon;
She comes more near the earth than she was wont,
And makes men mad. (v ii 107)

These are solid gems of poetry which lose little by divorce from their context: wherein they differ from the finest passages of *King Lear* or *Macbeth,* which are as wild flowers not to be uptorn from their rooted soil if they are to live. In these two quotations we should note how the human drama is thrown into sudden contrast and vivid unexpected relation with the tremendous concrete machinery of the universe, which is thought of in terms of individual heavenly bodies: 'sun' and 'moon'. The same effect is apparent in:

Nay, had she been true,
If Heaven would make me such another world
Of one entire and perfect chrysolite,
I'd not have sold her for it. (v ii 141)

Notice the single word 'chrysolite' with its outstanding and remote beauty: this is typcal of *Othello*.

The effect in such passages is primarily one of contrast. The vastness of the night sky, and its moving planets, or the earth itself – here conceived objectively as a solid, round, visualized object – these things, though thrown momentarily into sensible relation with the passions of man, yet remain vast, distant, separate, seen but not apprehended; something against which the dramatic movement may be silhouetted, but with which it cannot be merged. This poetic use of heavenly bodies serves to elevate the theme, to raise issues infinite and unknowable. Those bodies are not, however, implicit symbols of man's spirit, as in *King Lear*: they remain distinct, isolated phenomena, sublimely decorative to the end. In *Macbeth* and *King Lear* man commands the elements and the stars: they are part of him. Compare the above quotations from *Othello* with this from *King Lear*:

> You nimble lightnings, dart your blinding flames
> Into her scornful eyes! Infect her beauty,
> You fen-suck'd fogs, drawn by the powerful sun,
> To fall and blast her pride. (II iv 167)

This is typical: natural images are given a human value. They are insignificant, visually: their value is only that which they bring to the human passion which cries out to them. Their aesthetic grandeur, in and for themselves, is not relevant to the *King Lear* universe. So, too, Macbeth cries

> Stars, hide your fires;
> Let not light see my black and deep desires.
> (I iv 50)

And Lady Macbeth:

> Come, thick night,
> And pall thee in the dunnest smoke of Hell,
> That my keen knife see not the wound it makes,
> Nor Heaven peep through the blanket of the dark,
> To cry 'Hold, hold!' (I v 51)

Here, and in the *King Lear* extract, there is no clear visual effect as in *Othello*: tremendous images and suggestions are evoked only to be blurred as images by the more powerful passion which calls them into being. Images in *Macbeth* are thus continually vague, mastered by passion; apprehended, but not seen. In Othello's poetry they are concrete, detached; seen but not apprehended. We meet the same effect in:

> Like to the Pontic sea,
> Whose icy current and compulsive course
> Ne'er feels retiring ebb, but keeps due on
> To the Propontic and the Hellespont,
> Even so my bloody thoughts, with violent pace,
> Shall ne'er look back, ne'er ebb to humble love,
> Till that a capable and wide revenge
> Swallow them up. Now, by yond marble heaven,
> In the due reverence of a sacred vow
> I here engage my words. (III iii 454)

This is, indeed, a typical speech. The long comparison, explicitly made, where in *King Lear* or *Macbeth* a series of swiftly evolving metaphors would be more characteristic, is another example of the separateness, obtaining throughout *Othello*. There is no fusing of word with word, rather a careful juxtaposition of one word or image with another. And there are again the grand single words, 'Propontic', 'Hellespont', with their sharp, clear, consonant sounds, constituting defined aural solids typical of the *Othello* music: indeed, fine single words, especially proper names, are a characteristic of this play – Anthropophagi, Ottomites, Arabian trees, 'the base Indian', the Egyptian, Palestine, Mauretania, the Sagittary, Olympus, Mandragora, Othello, Desdemona. This is a rough assortment, not all used by Othello, but it points the Othello quality of rich, often expressly consonantal, outstanding words. Now Othello's prayer, with its 'marble heaven', is most typical and illustrative. One watches the figure of Othello silhouetted against a flat, solid, moveless sky: there is a plastic, static suggestion about the image. Compare it with a similar *King Lear* prayer:

O heavens,
If you do love old men, if your sweet sway
Allow obedience, if yourselves are old,
Make it your cause; send down and take my part!
(II iv 192)

Here we do not watch Lear: 'We are Lear.' There is no visual effect, no rigid subject–object relation between Lear and the 'heavens', nor any contrast, but an absolute unspatial unity of spirit. The heavens blend with Lear's prayer, each is part of the other. There is an intimate interdependence, not a mere juxtaposition. Lear thus identifies himself in kind with the heavens to which he addresses himself directly: Othello speaks of 'yond marble heaven', in the third person, and swears by it, does not pray to it. It is conceived as outside his interests.

This detached style, most excellent in point of clarity and stateliness, tends also to lose something in respect of power. At moments of great tension, the *Othello* style fails of a supreme effect. Capable of fine things quite unmatched in their particular quality in any other play, it nevertheless sinks sometimes to a studied artificiality, nerveless and without force. For example, Othello thinks of himself as:

...one whose subdued eyes,
Albeit unused to the melting mood,
Drop tears as fast as the Arabian trees
Their medicinal gum. (V ii 347)

Beside this we might place Macduff's

O I could play the woman with mine eyes
And braggart with my tongue! But, gentle heavens,
Cut short all intermission.... (IV iii 229)

... The *Othello* style is diffuse, leisurely, like a meandering river; the *Macbeth* style compressed, concentrated, and explosive; often jerky, leaping like a mountain torrent.... The *Othello* style does not compass the overpowering effects of *Macbeth* or *King Lear*: nor does it, as a rule, aim at them. At the most agonizing moments of Othello's story, however, there is apparent weakness: we find an exaggerated, false rhetoric.

There is a speech in *Othello* that begins in the typical restrained manner, but degenerates finally to what might almost be called bombast. It starts:

> Where should Othello go?
> Now, how dost thou look now? O ill-starr'd wench!
> Pale as thy smock! When we shall meet at compt,
> This look of thine will hurl my soul from Heaven,
> And fiends will snatch at it. Cold, cold, my girl!
> Even like thy chastity. (v ii 270)

Here we have the perfection of the *Othello* style. Concrete, visual, detached. Compare it with Lear's, 'Thou art a soul in bliss ...', where the effect, though perhaps more powerful and immediate, is yet vague, intangible, spiritualized. Now this speech, started in a style that can in its own way challenge that of *King Lear*, rapidly degenerates as Othello's mind is represented as collapsing under the extreme of anguish:

> O cursed, cursed slave! Whip me, ye devils,
> From the possession of this heavenly sight!
> Blow me about in winds! roast me in sulphur!
> Wash me in steep-down gulfs of liquid fire!
> O Desdemona! Desdemona! dead!
> Oh! Oh! Oh! (v ii 276)

There is a sudden reversal of poetic beauty: these lines lack cogency because they exaggerate rather than concentrate the emotion. Place beside these violent eschatological images the passage from *King Lear*:

And my poor fool is hang'd! No, no, no life!
Why should a dog, a horse, a rat have life,
And thou no breath at all? Thou'lt come no more,
Never, never, never, never, never!
Pray you, undo this button: thank you, sir.
Do you see this? Look on her, look, her lips,
Look there, look there! (v iii 307)

Notice by what rough, homely images the passion is transmitted – whch are as truly an integral part of the naturalism of *King Lear* as the mosaic and polished phrase, and the abstruse and picturesque allusion are, in its best passages, characteristic of Othello's speech. Thus the extreme, slightly exaggerated beauty of Othello's language is not maintained. This is even more true elsewhere. Othello, who usually luxuriates in deliberate and magnificent rhetoric, raves, falls in a trance:

> Lie with her! lie on her! We say lie on her, when they belie her. Lie with her! that's fulsome. Handkerchief – confessions – handkerchief! To confess, and be hanged for his labour; first, to be hanged, and then to confess – I tremble at it. Nature would not invest herself in such shadowing passion without some instruction. It is not words that shake me thus. Pish! Noses, ears, and lips. – Is't possible? – Confess – handkerchief! – O devil! (IV i 35)

Whereas Lear's madness never lacks artistic meaning, whereas its most extravagant and grotesque effects are presented with imaginative cogency, Othello can speak words like these. This is the Iago-spirit, the Iago-medicine, at work, like an acid eating into bright metal. This is the primary fact of Othello and therefore of the play: something of solid beauty is undermined, wedged open so that it exposes an extreme ugliness.

When Othello is represented as enduring loss of control he is, as Macbeth and Lear never are, ugly, idiotic; but when he has full control he attains an architectural stateliness of quarried speech, a silver rhetoric of a kind unique in Shakespeare:

It is the cause, it is the cause, my soul –
Let me not name it to you, you chaste stars! –
It is the cause. Yet I'll not shed her blood;
Nor scar that whiter skin of hers than snow,
And smooth as monumental alabaster.
Yet she must die, else she'll betray more men.
Put out the light, and then put out the light.
If I quench thee, thou flaming minister,
I can again thy former light restore,
Should I repent me: but once put out thy light,
Thou cunning'st pattern of excelling nature,
I know not where is that Promethean heat
That can thy light relume. When I have pluck'd the rose,
I cannot give it vital growth again,
It needs must wither: I'll smell it on the tree.
(v ii 1)

This is the noble *Othello* music: highly-coloured, rich in sound and phrase, stately. Each word solidifies as it takes its place in the pattern. This speech well illustrates the *Othello* style: the visual or tactile suggestion – 'whiter skin of hers than snow', 'smooth as monumental alabaster'; the slightly over-decorative phrase, 'flaming minister'; the momentary juxtaposition of humanity and the vast spaces of the night, the 'chaste stars'; the concrete imagery of 'thou cunning'st pattern of excelling nature', and the lengthy comparison of life with light; the presence of simple forward-flowing clarity of dignified statement and of simile in place of the super-logical welding of thought with molten thought as in the more compressed, agile, and concentrated poetry of *Macbeth* and *King Lear*; and the fine outstanding single word, 'Promethean'. In these respects Othello's speech is nearer the style of the aftermath of Elizabethan literature, the settled lava of that fiery eruption, which gave us the solid image of Marvell and the 'marmoreal phrase' of Browne: it is the most Miltonic thing in Shakespeare.

This peculiarity of style directs our interpretation in two ways. First, the tremendous reversal from extreme, almost over-decorative, beauty, to extreme ugliness – both of a kind unusual in Shakespeare – will be seen to reflect a primary truth about the play. That I will demonstrate later in my essay. Second, the concreteness and separation of image, word, or phrase, contrasting with the close-knit language elsewhere, suggests a proper approach to *Othello* which is not proper to *Macbeth* or *King Lear*. Separation is the rule throughout *Othello*. Whereas in *Macbeth* and *King Lear* we have one dominant atmosphere, built of a myriad subtleties of thought and phraseology entwining throughout, subduing our minds wholly to their respective visions, whereas each has a single quality, expresses as a whole a single statement, *Othello* is built rather of outstanding differences. In *Othello* all is silhouetted, defined, concrete. Instead of reading a unique, pervading, atmospheric suggestion – generally our key to interpretation of what happens within that atmosphere – we must here read the meaning of separate persons. The persons here are truly separate. Lear, Cordelia, Edmund all grow out of the *Lear* universe, all are levelled by its characteristic atmosphere, all blend with it and with each other, so that they are less closely and vividly defined. They lack solidity. Othello, Desdemona, Iago, however, are clearly and vividly separate. All here – but Iago – are solid, concrete. Contrast is raised to its highest pitch. Othello is statuesque, Desdemona most concretely human and individual, Iago, if not human or in any usual sense 'realistic', is quite unique. Within analysis of these three persons and their interaction lies the meaning of *Othello*. In *Macbeth* or *King Lear* we interpret primarily a singleness of vision. Here, confronted with a significant diversity, we must have regard to the essential relation existing between the three main personal conceptions. Interpretation must be based not on unity but differentiation. Therefore I shall pursue an examination of this triple symbolism; which analysis will finally resolve the difficulty of Othello's speech, wavering as it does between what at first sight appear an almost artificial beauty and an equally inartistic ugliness.

Othello radiates a world of romantic, heroic, and picturesque adventure. All about him is highly coloured. He is a Moor; he is noble and generally respected; he is proud in the riches of his achievement. Now his prowess as a soldier is emphasized. His arms have spent 'their dearest action in the tented field' (I iii 85)....
But we also meet a curious discrepancy. Othello tells us:

> Rude am I in my speech,
> And little bless'd with the soft phrase of peace.
> (I iii 81)

Yet the dominant quality in this play is the exquisitely moulded language, the noble cadence and chiselled phrase, of Othello's poetry. Othello's speech, therefore, reflects not a soldier's language, but the quality of soldiership in all its glamour of romantic adventure; it holds an imaginative realism. It has a certain exotic beauty, is a storied and romantic treasure-house of rich, colourful experiences....
Swords are vivid, spiritualized things to Othello. There is his famous line:

> Keep up your bright swords, for the dew will rust them. (I ii 59)

And in the last scene, he says:

> I have another weapon in this chamber;
> It is a sword of Spain, the ice-brook's temper.
> (V ii 251)

In his address at the end, he speaks of himself as

one whose hand,
Like the base Indian, threw a pearl away
Richer than all his tribe. (v ii 345)

His tears flow as the gum from 'Arabian trees' (v ii 349); he recounts how in Aleppo he smote 'a malignant and a turban'd Turk' (v ii 352) for insulting Venice. Finally there is his noble apostrophe to his lost 'occupation':

Farewell the plumed troop and the big wars,
That make ambition virtue! O, farewell!
Farewell the neighing steed and the shrill trump,
The spirit-stirring drum, the ear-piercing fife,
The royal banner and all quality,
Pride, pomp, and circumstance of glorious war!
And, O you mortal engines, whose rude throats
The immortal Jove's dread clamours counterfeit,
Farewell! Othello's occupation 's gone. (III iii 350)

Again, we have the addition of phrase to separate phrase, rather than the interdependence, the evolution of thought from thought, the clinging mesh of close-bound suggestions of other plays. This noble eulogy of war is intrinsic to the conception. War is in Othello's blood. When Desdemona accepts him, she knows she must not be 'a moth of peace' (I iii 258). Othello is a compound of highly-coloured, romantic adventure – he is himself 'coloured' – and war; together with a great pride and a great faith in those realities. His very life is dependent on a fundamental belief in the validity and nobility of human action – with, perhaps, a strong tendency towards his own achievements in particular. Now war, in Shakespeare, is usually a positive spiritual value, like love. There is reference to the soldiership of the protagonist in all the plays analysed in my present treatment. Soldiership is almost the condition of nobility, and so the Shakespearian hero is usually a soldier. Therefore Othello, with reference to the Shakespearian universe, becomes automatically a symbol of faith in human values of love, of war, of romance in a wide and sweeping sense. He is, as it were, conscious of all he stands for: from the first to the last he loves his own romantic history. He is, like Troilus, dedicate to these values, has faith and pride in both. Like Troilus he is conceived as extraordinarily direct, simple, 'credulous' (IV i 46). Othello, as he appears in the action of the play, may be considered the high-priest of human endeavour, robed in the vestments of romance, whom we watch serving in the temple of war at the altar of love's divinity.

Desdemona is his divinity. She is, at the same time, warmly human. There is a certain domestic femininity about her. She is 'a maiden never bold' (I iii 94). We hear that 'the house affairs' (had Cordelia any?) drew her often from Othello's narrative (I iii 147). But she asks to hear the whole history:

> I did consent,
> And often did beguile her of her tears,
> When I did speak of some distressful stroke
> That my youth suffered. My story being done,
> She gave me for my pains a world of sighs:
> She swore, in faith, 'twas strange, 'twas passing strange,
> 'Twas pitiful, 'twas wondrous pitiful:
> She wish'd she had not heard it, yet she wish'd
> That heaven had made her such a man.
> (I iii 155)

The same domesticity and gentleness is apparent throughout. She talks of 'to-night at supper' (III iii 57) or 'to-morrow dinner' (III iii 58); she is typically feminine in her attempt to help Cassio, and her pity for him. This is how she describes her suit to Othello:

> Why, this is not a boon;
> 'Tis as I should entreat you wear your gloves,
> Or feed on nourishing dishes, or keep you warm,
> Or sue to you to do a peculiar profit
> To your own person ... (III iii 76)

– a speech reflecting a world of sex-contrast. She would bind Othello's head with her handkerchief – that handkerchief which is to become a terrific symbol of Othello's jealousy. The *Othello* world is eminently domestic, and Desdemona expressly feminine. We hear of her needlework (IV i 197), her fan, gloves, mask (IV ii 8). In the exquisite willow-song scene, we see her with her maid, Emilia. Emilia gives her 'her nightly wearing' (IV iii 16). Emilia says she has laid on her bed the 'wedding-sheets' (IV ii 104) Desdemona asked for. Then there is the willow-song, brokenly sung whilst Emilia 'unpins' (IV iii 34) Desdemona's dress:

> My mother had a maid called Barbara:
> She was in love, and he she loved proved mad
> And did forsake her.... (IV iii 26)

The extreme beauty and pathos of this scene are largely dependent on the domesticity of it. *Othello* is eminently a domestic tragedy. But this element in the play is yet to be related to another more universal element. Othello is concretely human, so is Desdemona. Othello is very much the typical middle-aged bachelor entering matrimony late in life, but he is also, to transpose a phrase of Iago's, a symbol of human – especially masculine – 'purpose, courage, and valour' (IV ii 218), and, in a final judgement, is seen to represent the idea of human faith and value in a very wide sense. Now Desdemona, also very human, with an individual domestic feminine charm and simplicity, is yet also a symbol of woman in general daring the unknown seas of marriage with the mystery of man. Beyond this, in the far flight of a transcendental interpretation, it is clear that she becomes a symbol of man's ideal, the supreme value of love. At the limit of the series of wider and wider suggestions which appear from imaginative contemplation of a poetic symbol she is to be equated with the divine principle. In one scene of *Othello*, and one only, direct poetic symbolism breaks across the vividly human, domestic world of this play.* As everything in *Othello* is separated, defined, so the plot itself is in two distinct geographical divisions: Venice and Cyprus. Desdemona leaves the safety and calm of her home for the stormy voyage to Cyprus and the tempest of the following tragedy. Iago's plot begins to work in the second part. The storm scene, between the two parts, is important.

Storms are continually symbols of tragedy in Shakespeare. This scene contains some most vivid imaginative effects, among them passages of fine storm-poetry of the usual kind:

> For do but stand upon the foaming shore,
> The chidden billow seems to pelt the clouds;
> The wind-shak'd surge, with high and monstrous
>   mane,
> Seems to cast water on the burning bear,
> And quench the guards of the ever-fixed pole:
> I never did like molestation view,
> On the enchafed flood. (II i 11)

This storm-poetry is here closely associated with the human element. And in this scene where direct storm-symbolism occurs it is noteworthy that the figures of Desdemona and Othello are both strongly idealized:

> *Cassio.* Tempests themselves, high seas and howling
>   winds,
>   The gutter'd rocks and congregated sands –
>   Traitors ensteep'd to clog the guiltless keel –
>   As having sense of beauty, do omit
>   Their mortal natures, letting go safely by
>   The divine Desdemona.
> *Montano.* What is she?
> *Cassio.* She that I spake of, our great captain's
>   captain,
>   Left in the conduct of the bold Iago,

* But note too the significance of the magic handkerchief *as both a symbol of domestic sanctity and the play's one link with the supernatural* (1947).

Whose footing here anticipates our thoughts
A se'nnight's speed. Great Jove, Othello guard,
And swell his sail with thine own powerful breath,
That he may bless this bay with his tall ship,
Make love's quick pants in Desdemona's arms,
Give renewed fire to our extincted spirits,
And bring all Cyprus comfort!
Enter Desdemona, &c.
O, behold,
The riches of the ship is come on shore!
Ye men of Cyprus, let her have your knees.
Hail to thee, lady! and the grace of Heaven,
Before, behind thee, and on every hand,
Enwheel thee round! (II i 68)

Desdemona is thus endued with a certain transcendent quality of beauty and grace. She 'paragons description and wild fame' says Cassio: she is

One that excels the quirks of blazoning pens,
And in the essential vesture of creation
Does tire the ingener. (II i 63)

And Othello enters the port of Cyprus as a hero coming to 'bring comfort', to 'give renewed fire' to men. The entry of Desdemona and that of Othello are both heralded by discharge of guns: which both merges finely with the tempest-symbolism and the violent stress and excitement of the scene as a whole, and heightens our sense of the warrior nobility of the protagonist and his wife, subdued as she is 'to the very quality' of her lord (I iii 253). Meeting Desdemona, he speaks:

Othello. O my fair warrior!
Desdemona. My dear Othello!
Othello. It gives me wonder great as my content
To see you here before me. O my soul's joy!
If after every tempest come such calms,
May the winds blow till they have waken'd death!
And let the labouring bark climb hills of seas

> Olympus-high and duck again as low
> As Hell's from Heaven! If it were now to die,
> 'Twere now to be most happy; for, I fear,
> My soul hath her content so absolute
> That not another comfort like to this
> Succeeds in unknown fate. (II i 185)

This is the harmonious marriage of true and noble minds. Othello, Desdemona, and their love are here apparent, in this scene of storm and reverberating discharge of cannon, as things of noble and conquering strength: they radiate romantic valour. Othello is essential man in all his prowess and protective strength; Desdemona essential woman, gentle, loving, brave in trust of her warrior husband. The war is over. The storm of sea or bruit of cannonade are powerless to hurt them: yet there is another storm brewing in the venomed mind of Iago. Instead of merging with and accompanying tragedy the storm here is thus contrasted with the following tragic events: as usual in *Othello*, contrast and separation take the place of fusion and unity. This scene is thus a microcosm of the play, reflecting its action. Colours which are elsewhere softly toned are here splashed vividly on the play's canvas. Here especially Othello appears a prince of heroes. Desdemona is lit by a divine feminine radiance: both are transfigured. They are shown as coming safe to land, by Heaven's 'grace', triumphant, braving war and tempestuous seas, guns thundering their welcome. The reference of all this, on the plane of high poetic symbolism, to the play as a whole is evident.

Against these two Iago pits his intellect. In this scene too Iago declares himself with especial clarity:

> O gentle lady, do not put me to't;
> For I am nothing, if not critical. (II i 118)

His conversation with Desdemona reveals his philosophy. Presented under the cloak of fun, it exposes nevertheless his attitude to life: that of the cynic.

Roderigo is his natural companion: the fool is a convenient implement, and at the same time continual food for his philosophy. Othello and Desdemona are radiant, beautiful: Iago opposes them, critical intellectual. Like cold steel his cynic skill will run through the warm body of their love. Asked to praise Desdemona, he draws a picture of womanly goodness in a vein of mockery; and concludes:

> *Iago*. She was a wight if ever such wight were –
> *Desdemona*. To do what?
> *Iago*. To suckle fools and chronicle small beer.
> (II i 158)

Here is his reason for hating Othello's and Desdemona's love: he hates their beauty. to him a meaningless, stupid thing. That is Iago. Cynicism is his philosophy, his very life, his 'motive' in working Othello's ruin. The play turns on this theme: the cynical intellect pitted against a lovable humanity transfigured by qualities of heroism and grace. As Desdemona and Othello embrace he says:

> O you are well tuned now!
> But I'll set down the pegs that make this music,
> As honest as I am. (II i 202)

'Music' is apt: we remember Othello's rich harmony of words. Against the *Othello* music Iago concentrates all the forces of cynic villainy.

Iago's cynicism is recurrent:

> Virtue! a fig! 'tis in ourselves that we are thus or
> thus.... (I iii 323)

Love to him is

> ... merely a lust of the blood and a permission of the
> will. (I iii 339)

He believes Othello's and Desdemona's happiness will be short-lived, since he puts no faith in the validity of love. Early in the play he tells Roderigo:

> It cannot be that Desdemona should long continue her love to the Moor . . . nor he his to her. . . . These Moors are changeable in their wills . . . the food that to him now is as luscious as locusts, shall be to him shortly as bitter as coloquintida. She must change for youth: when she is sated with his body, she will find the error of her choice: she must have change, she must. (I iii 347)

This is probably Iago's sincere belief, his usual attitude to love: he is not necessarily deceiving Roderigo. After this, when he is alone, we hear that he suspects Othello with his own wife: nor are we surprised. And, finally, his own cynical beliefs suggest to him a way of spiting Othello. He thinks of Cassio:

> After some time, to abuse Othello's ear
> That he is too familiar with his wife.
> (I iii 401)

The order is important: Iago first states his disbelief in Othello's and Desdemona's continued love, and next thinks of a way of precipitating its end. That is, he puts his cynicism into action. The same rhythmic sequence occurs later. Iago witnesses Cassio's meeting with Desdemona at Cyprus, and comments as follows:

> He takes her by the palm: ay, well said, whisper: with as little a web as this will I ensnare as great a fly as Cassio. Ay, smile upon her, do; I will gyve thee in thine own courtship . . . . (II i 168)

Iago believes Cassio loves Desdemona. He has another cynical conversation with Roderigo as to Desdemona's chances of finding satisfaction with Othello, and the probability of her love for Cassio (II i 223–79). A kiss, to Iago, cannot be 'courtesy': it is

> Lechery, by this hand; an index and obscure prologue to the history of lust and foul thoughts.
> (II i 265)

Iago is sincere enough and means what he says. Cynicism is the key to his mind and actions. After Roderigo's departure, he again refers to his suspicions of Othello – and Cassio too – with his own wife. He asserts definitely – and here there is no Roderigo to impress – his belief in Cassio's guilt:

> That Cassio loves her, I do well believe it;
> That she loves him, 'tis apt and of great credit.
> (II i 298)

In this soliloquy he gets his plans clearer: again, they are suggested by what he believes to be truth. I do not suggest that Iago lacks conscious villainy: far from it. Besides, in another passage he shows that he is aware of Desdemona's innocence (IV i 48). But it is important that we observe how his attitude to life casts the form and figure of his meditated revenge. His plan arises out of the cynical depths of his nature. When, at the end, he says, 'I told him what I thought' (V ii 174), he is speaking at least a half-truth. He hates the romance of Othello and the loveliness of Desdemona because he is by nature the enemy of these things. Cassio, he says,

> hath a daily beauty in his life
> That makes mine ugly. (V i 19)

This is his 'motive' throughout: other suggestions are surface deep only. He is cynicism loathing beauty, refusing to allow its existence. Hence the venom of his plot: the plot is Iago – both are ultimate, causeless, self-begotten. Iago is cynicism incarnate and projected into action.

Iago is thus utterly devilish: there is no weakness in his casing armour of unrepentant villainy. He is a kind of Mephistopheles, closely equivalent to Goethe's devil, the two possessing the same qualities of mockery and easy cynicism. Thus he is called a 'hellish villain' by Lodovico (v ii 367), a 'demi-devil' by Othello (v ii 300). Othello says:

I look down towards his feet; but that 's a fable.
If that thou be'est a devil, I cannot kill thee.
(v ii 285)

Iago himself recognizes a kinship:

Hell and night
Must bring this monstrous birth to the world's sight.
(I iii 409)

And,

Divinity of Hell!
When devils will the blackest sins put on,
They do suggest at first with heavenly shows
As I do now. (II iii 359)

He knows that his 'poison' (III iii 326) will 'burn like the mines of sulphur' (III iii 330) in Othello. Thus Iago is, to Othello, the antithesis of Desdemona: the relation is that of the spirit of denial to the divine principle. Desdemona 'plays the god' (II iii 356) with Othello: if she is false, 'Heaven mocks itself' (III iii 278). During the action, as Iago's plot succeeds, her essential divinity changes, for Othello, to a thing hideous and devilish – that is to its antithesis:

Her name that was as fresh
As Dian's visage, is now begrimed and black
As mine own face. (III iii 387)

She is now 'devil' (IV i 252, 255) or 'the fair devil' (III iii 479); her hand, a 'sweating devil' (III iv 43); the 'devils themselves' will fear to seize her for her heavenly looks (IV ii 35). Thus Iago, himself a kind of devil, insidiously eats his way into this world of romance, chivalry, nobility. The word 'devil' occurs frequently in the latter acts: devils are alive here, ugly little demons of black disgrace. They swarm over the mental horizon of the play, occurring frequently. Iago is directly or indirectly their author and originator. 'Devil', 'Hell', 'damnation' – these words are recurrent, and continually juxtaposed to thoughts of 'Heaven', prayer, angels. We are clearly set amid 'Heaven and men and devils' (v ii 219). Such terms are related here primarily to sexual impurity. In *Othello,* pure love is the supreme good; impurity damnation. This pervading religious tonal significance relating to infidelity explains lines such as:

> Turn thy complexion there,
> Patience, thou young and rose-lipped cherubin –
> Ay, there, look grim as Hell! (IV ii 61)

Othello addresses Emilia:

> You, mistress,
> That have the office opposite to Saint Peter,
> And keep the gate of Hell! (IV ii 89)

Here faithful love is to be identified with the divine, the 'heavenly'; unfaithful love, or the mistrust which imagines it, or the cynic that gives birth to that imagination – all these are to be identified with the devil. The hero is set between the forces of Divinity and Hell. The forces of Hell win and pure love lies slain. Therefore Othello cries to 'devils' to whip him from that 'heavenly' sight (v ii 276). He knows himself to have been entrapped by hell-forces. The Iago–Devil association is of importance.

It will be remembered that *Othello* is a play of concrete forms. This world is a world of visual images, colour, and romance. It will also be clear that the mesh of devil-references I have just suggested show a mental horizon black, formless, colourless. They contrast with the solid, chiselled, enamelled *Othello* style of elsewhere. This devil-world is insubstantial, vague, negative. Now on the plane of personification we see that Othello and Desdemona are concrete, moulded of flesh and blood, warm. Iago contrasts with them metaphysically as well as morally: he is unlimited, formless villainy. He is the spirit of denial, wholly negative. He never has visual reality. He is further blurred by the fact of his being something quite different from what he appears to the others. Is he to look like a bluff soldier, or Mephistopheles? He is a different kind of being from Othello and Desdemona: he belongs to a different world. They, by their very existence, assert the positive beauty of created forms – hence Othello's perfected style of speech, his strong human appeal, his faith in creation's values of love and war. This world of created forms, this sculptured and yet pulsing beauty, the Iago-spirit undermines, poisons, disintegrates. Iago is a demon of cynicism, colourless, formless, in a world of colours, shapes, and poetry's music. Of all these he would create chaos. Othello's words are apt:

> Excellent wretch! Perdition catch my soul
> But I do love thee! And when I love thee not,
> Chaos is come again. (III iii 90)

Chaos indeed. Iago works at the foundations of human values. Cassio is a soldier: he ruins him as a soldier, makes him drunk. So he ruins both Othello's love and warrior-heart. He makes him absurd, ugly. Toward the end of the play there is hideous suggestion. We hear of 'cords, knives, poison' (III iii 389), of lovers 'as prime as goats, as hot as monkeys' (III iii 404); we meet Bianca, the whore, told by Cassio to 'throw her vile guesses in the Devil's teeth' (III iv 183); there are Othello's incoherent mutterings, 'Pish! Noses, ears and lips!' (IV i 43), he will 'chop' Desdemona 'into messes' (IV i 210); she reminds him of 'foul toads' (IV ii 60). Watching Cassio, he descends to this:

> O! I see that nose of yours, but not the dog I shall throw it to. (IV i 144)

Othello strikes Desdemona, behaves like a raging beast. 'Fire and brimstone!' (IV i 246) he cries, and again, 'Goats and monkeys!' (IV i 274). 'Heaven stops the nose' at Desdemona's impurity (IV ii 76). Othello in truth behaves like 'a beggar in his drink' (IV ii 120). In all these phrases I would emphasize not the sense and dramatic relevance alone, but the suggestion – the accumulative effect of ugliness, hellishness, idiocy, negation. It is a formless, colourless essence, insidiously undermining a world of concrete, visual, richly-toned forms. That is the Iago-spirit embattled against the domesticity, the romance, the idealized humanity of the *Othello* world.

Here, too, we find the reason for the extreme contrast of Othello's two styles: one exotically beautiful, the other blatantly absurd, ugly. There is often no dignity in Othello's rage. There is not meant to be. Iago would make discord of the *Othello* music. Thus at his first conquest he filches something of Othello's style and uses it himself:

> Not poppy, nor mandragora,
> Nor all the drowsy syrups of the world,
> Shall ever medicine thee to that sweet sleep
> Which thou owed'st yesterday. (III iii 331)

To him Othello's pride in his life-story and Desdemona's admiration were ever stupid:

> Mark me with what violence she first loved the Moor, but for bragging and telling her fantastical lies: and will she love him still for prating? (II i 225)

Iago, 'nothing if not critical', speaks some truth of Othello's style – it is 'fantastical'. As I have shown, it is somewhat over-decorative, highly-coloured. The dramatic value of this style now appears. In fact, a proper understanding of Othello's style reveals Iago's 'motive' so often questioned. There is something sentimental in Othello's language, in Othello. Iago is pure cynicism. That Iago should scheme – in this dramatic symbolism forged in terms of interacting persons – to undermine Othello's faith in himself, his wife, and his 'occupation', is inevitable. Logically, the cynic must oppose the sentimentalist: dramatically, he works his ruin by deceit and deception. That Othello often just misses tragic dignity is the price of his slightly strained emotionalism. Othello loves emotion for its own sake, luxuriates in it, like Richard II. As ugly and idiot ravings, disjointed and with no passionate dignity even, succeed Othello's swell and flood of poetry, Iago's triumph seems complete. The honoured warrior, rich in strength and experience, noble in act and repute, lies in a trance, nerveless, paralysed by the Iago-conception:

> Work on, my medicine, work. (IV i 45)

But Iago's victory is not absolute. During the last scene, Othello is a nobly tragic figure. His ravings are not final: he rises beyond them. He slays Desdemona finally not so much in rage, as for 'the cause' (V ii 1). He slays her in love. Though Desdemona fails him, his love, homeless, 'perplexed in the extreme' (V ii 345), endures. He will kill her and 'love her after' (V ii 19). In that last scene, too, he utters the grandest of his poetry. The Iago-spirit never finally envelops him, masters him, disintegrates his soul. Those gem-like miniatures of poetic movement quoted at the start of my essay are among Othello's last words. His vast love has, it is true, failed in a domestic world. But now symbols of the wide beauty of the universe enrich his thoughts: the 'chaste stars', and sun and moon', the 'affrighted globe', the world 'of one entire and perfect chrysolite' that may not buy a Desdemona's love. At the end we know that Othello's fault is simplicity alone. He is, indeed, 'a gull, a dolt' (V ii 161); he loves 'not wisely but too well' (V ii 343). His simple faith in himself endures:

and at the end, he takes just pride in recalling his honourable service.

In this essay I have attempted to expose the underlying thought of the play. Interpretation here is not easy, nor wholly satisfactory. As all within *Othello* – save the Iago-theme – is separated, differentiated, solidified, so the play itself seems at first to be divorced from wider issues, a lone thing of meaningless beauty in the Shakespearian universe, solitary, separate, unyielding and chaste as the moon. It is unapproachable, yields itself to no easy mating with our minds. Its thought does not readily mesh with our thought. We can visualize it, admire its concrete felicities of phrase and image, the mosaic of its language, the sculptural outline of its effects, the precision and chastity of its form. But one cannot be lost in it, subdued to it, enveloped by it, as one is drenched and refreshed by the elemental cataracts of *King Lear*; one cannot be intoxicated by it as by the rich wine of *Antony and Cleopatra*. *Othello* is essentially outside us, beautiful with a lustrous, planetary beauty. Yet the Iago-conception is of a different kind from the rest of the play. This conception alone, if no other reason existed, would point the necessity of an intellectual interpretation. So we see the Iago-spirit gnawing at the root of all the *Othello* values, the *Othello* beauties; he eats into the core and heart of this romantic world, worms his way into its solidity, rotting it, poisoning it. Once this is clear, the whole play begins to have meaning. On the plane of dramatic humanity, we see a story of the cynic intriguing to ruin the soldier and his love. On the plane of poetic conception, in matters of technique, style, personification – there we see a spirit of negation, colourless, and undefined, attempting to make chaos of a world of stately, architectural, and exquisitely coloured forms. The two styles of Othello's speech illustrate this. Thus the different technique of the Othello and Iago conceptions is intrinsic with the plot of the play: in them we have the spirit of negation set against the spirit of creation. That is why Iago is undefined, devisualized, inhuman, in a play of consummate skill in concrete imagery and vivid human delineation. He is a colourless and ugly thing in a world of colour and harmony. His failure lies in this: in the final scene, at the moment of his complete triumph, Emilia dies for her mistress to the words of Desdemona's willow-song, and the *Othello* music itself sounds with a nobler cadence, a richer flood of harmonies, a more selfless and universalized flight of the imagination than before. The beauties of the *Othello* world are not finally disintegrated: they make 'a swan-like end, fading in music'.

SOURCE: *The Wheel of Fire* (1930).

ADDITIONAL NOTE (1947)

Any valuable discussions of Othello's physical appearance and general status as a 'noble Moor' must take full account of Morocco's self-description in *The Merchant of Venice*. Imaginatively, the two conceptions are almost identical, the one being a first sketch of the other.

For the Handkerchief, see my note on p. 109; and also my *Principles of Shakespearian Production*.

William Empson

HONEST IN *OTHELLO* (1951)

The fifty-two uses of *honest* and *honesty* in *Othello* are a very queer business; there is no other play in which Shakespeare worries a word like that. *King Lear* uses *fool* nearly as often but does not treat it as a puzzle, only as a source of profound metaphors. In *Othello* divergent uses of the key word are found for all the main characters; even the attenuated clown plays on it; the unchaste Bianca, for instance, snatches a moment to claim that she is more honest than Emilia the thief of the handkerchief; and with all the variety of use the ironies on the word mount up steadily to the end. Such is the general power of the writing that this is not obtrusive, but if all but the phrases involving *honest* were in the style of Ibsen the effect would be a symbolical charade. Everybody calls Iago honest once or twice, but with Othello it becomes an obsession; at the crucial moment just before Emilia exposes Iago he keeps howling the word out. The general effect has been fully recognised by critics, but it looks as if there is something to be found about the word itself.

What Shakespeare hated in the word, I believe, was a peculiar use, at once hearty and individualist, which was then common among raffish low people but did not become upper-class till the Restoration; here as in Iago's heroic couplets the play has a curious effect of prophecy. But to put it like this is no doubt to oversimplify; the Restoration use, easy to feel though hard to define, seems really different from its earlier parallels, and in any case does not apply well to Iago. I want here to approach the play without taking for granted the previous analysis. But I hope it has become obvious that the word was in the middle of a rather complicated process of change, and that what emerged from it was a sort of jovial cult of independence. At some stage of the development (whether by the date of *Othello* or not) the word came to have in it a covert assertion that the man who accepts the natural desires, who does not live by principle, will be fit for such warm uses of *honest* as imply 'generous' and 'faithful to friends', and to believe this is to disbelieve the Fall of Man. Thus the word, apart from being complicated, also came to raise large issues, and it is not I think a wild fancy to suppose that Shakespeare could feel the way it was going.

Four columns of *honest* in the Shakespeare Concordance show that he never once allows the word a simple hearty use between equals. Some low characters get near it, but they are made to throw in contempt. 'An honest fellow enough, and one that loves quails' is said by Thersites in contempt for Ajax; 'honest good fellows' is said by the Nurse in Romeo, but of minstrels that she is turning away; 'as honest a true fellow as any in Bohemia' is from Prince Cloten and to a shepherd; 'I am with thee here and the goats, as the most capricious poet, honest Ovid, was mong the Goths' gets its joke from making the clown patronise Ovid. The nearest case is from Desdemona:

EMIL.: *I warrant it grieves my husband*
As if the case were his.
DES.: *Oh, that's an honest fellow.*

But Emilia is butting into the talk with Cassio, and Desdemona, in this careless reply to silence her, has a feeling that Iago though reliable and faithful is her social inferior. This indeed is a sufficient reason why Iago talks with irony about the admitted fact that he is 'honest'; the patronising use carried an obscure social insult as well as a hint of stupidity. Critics have discussed what the social status of Iago and Emilia would actually be, and have succeeded in making clear that the posts of ancient and gentlewoman-in-waiting might be held by people of very varying status; the audience must use its own judgement. The hints seem to place Iago and his wife definitely enough well below Desdemona but well above Ancient Pistol, say. Now at the same date as the refusal by Shakespeare to employ a flat hearty use of the word, there are uses by Dekker (for example) which only differ from the Restoration ones by coming from people of lower rank or bad reputation. One need not say that Shakespeare always had a conscious policy about the word (more likely the flat hearty use bored him; it was a blank space where one might have had a bit of word play) but his uses of it in *Othello,* when his imagination began to work on the loathsome possibilities of this familiar bit of nonsense, are consistent with his normal practice.

Most people would agree with what Bradley, for example, implied, that the way everybody calls Iago honest amounts to a criticism of the word itself; that is, Shakespeare means 'a bluff forthright manner, and amusing talk, which get a man called honest, may go with extreme dishonesty'. Or indeed that this is treated as normal, and the satire is on our nature not on language. But they would probably maintain that Iago is not honest and does not think himself so, and only calls himself so as a lie or an irony. It seems to me, if you leave the matter there, that there is much to be said for what the despised Rymer decided, when the implications of the hearty use of *honest* had become simpler and more clear-cut. He said that the play is ridiculous, because that sort of villain (silly-clever, full of secret schemes, miscalculating about people) does not get mistaken for that sort of honest man. This if true is of course a plain fault, whatever you think about 'character-analysis'. It is no use taking short cuts in these things, and I should fancy that what Rymer said had a large truth when he said it, and also that Iago was a plausible enough figure in his own time. The only main road into this baffling subject is to find how the characters actually use the term and thereby think about themselves.

I must not gloss over the fact that Iago once uses the word to say that he proposes to tell Othello lies:

> *The Moor is of a free and open nature,*
> *And thinks men honest that but seem to be so.*

This is at the end of the first act. And indeed, the first use of the word in the play seems also to mean that Iago does not think himself honest. In his introductory scene with Roderigo, he says of the subservient type of men 'whip me such honest knaves'; they are opposed to the independent men like himself – 'these fellows have some soul'. Later there is a trivial use of the word by Brabantio, but the next important ones do not come till near the end of the act. Then Othello twice calls Iago honest; Iago immediately (to insist on the irony) has a second meeting for plots with Roderigo, and then in soliloquy tells the audience he will cheat Roderigo too. Next he brings out the two lines just quoted; he is enumerating the conditions of his problem, and the dramatic purpose, one may say, is to make certain that nobody in the audience has missed the broad point. The act then closes with 'I have it' and the triumphant claim that he has invented the plot. Even here, I think, there is room for an ironical tone in Iago's use of *honest*; he can imply that Othello's notion of honesty is crude as well as his judgements about which people exemplify it. For that matter, Iago may simply be speaking about Cassio, not about himself. He has just said that Cassio is framed to make women false, and he certainly regards the virtues of Cassio as part of his superficial and over-rewarded charm of manner. But I think that, even so, Iago has himself somewhere in view; to claim that he did not would be overstraining my argument. The introductory phrase 'honest knaves' is of course a direct irony (made clear by contradiction); it can only mean that Iago has a different idea of honesty from the one that these knaves have. To be sure, you may be meant to think that he is lying by implication, but even so, this is the lie that he must be supposed to tell. However, I do not see that the uses at either end of the act put forward definite alternative meanings for the word; they lay the foundations by making it prominent. It is then, so to speak, 'in play' and is used with increasing frequency. The first act has five uses; the second eleven; the third twenty-three; and the last two only six and seven. One might argue that the character of Iago is established in the first act before the verbal ironies are applied to it, since 'honest knaves' is only a sort of blank cheque; but even so we learn a good deal more about him later.

Both Iago and Othello oppose honesty to mere truth-telling:

> OTH.: *I know, Iago,*
> *Thy honesty and love doth mince this matter,*
> *Making it light to Cassio....*
> IAGO: *It were not for your quiet, nor your good,*
> *Nor for my manhood, honesty, or wisdom*
> *To let you know my thoughts.*

No doubt the noun tends to be more old-fashioned than the adjective, but anyway the old 'honourable' sense is as broad and vague as the new slang one; it was easy enough to be puzzled by the word. Iago means partly 'faithful to friends', which would go with the Restoration use, but partly I think 'chaste', the version normally used of women; what he has to say is improper. Certainly one cannot simply treat his version of *honest* as the Restoration one – indeed, the part of the snarling critic involves a rather Puritanical view, at any rate towards other people. It is the two notions of being ready to blow the gaff on other people and frank to yourself about your own desires that seem to me crucial about Iago; they grow on their own, independently of the hearty feeling that would normally humanize them; though he can be a good companion as well.

One need not look for a clear sense when he toys with the word about Cassio; the question is how it came to be so mystifying. But I think a queer kind of honesty is maintained in Iago through all the puzzles he contrives; his emotions are always expressed directly, and it is only because they are clearly genuine ('These stops of thine', Othello tells him, 'are close relations, working from the heart') that he can mislead Othello as to their cause.

OTH.: *Is he not honest?* (Faithful, etc.)
IAGO: *Honest, my lord?* (Not stealing, etc. Shocked)
OTH.: *Ay, honest,* ('Why repeat? The word is clear enough.')
IAGO: *My lord, for aught I know....* ('In some sense.')
IAGO: *For Michael Cassio*
I dare be sworn I think that he is honest.
OTH.: *I think so too.*
IAGO: *Men should be what they seem,*
Or, those that be not, would they might seem none.
OTH.: *Certain, men should be what they seem.*
IAGO: *Why then, I think that Cassio's an honest man.*

Othello has just said that Cassio 'went between them very oft', so Iago now learns that Cassio lied to him in front of Brabantio's house when he pretended to know nothing about the marriage. Iago feels he has been snubbed,* as too coarse to be trusted in such a manner, and he takes immediate advantage of his discomposure. The point of his riddles is to get 'not hypocritical' –

* Cassio does not call Iago *honest* till he can use the word warmly (II iii 108); till then he calls him 'good Iago' (II i 97, II iii 34) – apparently a less obtrusive form of the same trick of patronage. Possibly as they have been rivals for his present job he feels it more civil to keep his distance. However the social contempt which he holds in check is hinted jovially to Desdemona (II i 165) and comes out plainly when he is drunk; Iago returns the 'good' to him and is firmly snubbed for it as not a 'man of quality' (II iii 108).

'frank about his own nature' accepted as the relevan sense; Iago will readily call him honest on that basis and Othello cannot be reassured. 'Chaste' (the sens normally used of women) Cassio is not, but he is 'no a hypocrite' about Bianca. Iago indeed, despises hi for letting her make a fool of him in public; for tha and for other reasons (Cassio is young and without ex perience) Iago can put a contemptuous tone into th word; the feeling is genuine, but not the sense it ma imply. This gives room for a hint that Cassio has bee 'frank' to Iago in private about more things than ma honestly be told. I fancy too, that the idea of 'not being men' gives an extra twist. Iago does not think Cassi manly nor that it is specially manly to be chaste; thi allows him to agree that Cassio may be honest in the female sense about Desdemona and still keep a tone which seems to deny it – if he is, after so much encouragement, he must be 'effeminate' (there is a strong idea of 'manly' in *honest*, and an irony on that gives its opposite). Anyway, Iago can hide what reservations he makes but show that he makes reservations; this suggests an embarrassed defence – 'Taking a broad view, with the world as it is, and Cassio my friend, I can decently call him honest.' This forces home the Restoration idea – 'an honest dog of a fellow, straightforward about women', and completes the suspicion. It is a bad piece of writing unless you are keyed up for the shifts of the word.

The play with the feminine version is doubtful here, but he certainly does it the other way round about Desdemona, where it had more point; in the best case it is for his own amusement when alone.

And what's he then that says I play the villain?
When this advice is free I give and honest,
Probal to thinking, and indeed the course
To win the Moor again? For 'tis most easy
The inclining Desdemona to subdue
In any honest suit. She's framed as fruitful
As the free elements.

Easy, inclining, fruitful, free all push the word the same way, from 'chaste' to 'flat, frank, and natural'; all turn the ironical admission of her virtue into a positive insult against her. The delight in juggling with the word here is close to the Machiavellian interest in plots for their own sake, which Iago could not resist and allowed to destroy him. But a good deal of the 'motive-hunting' of the soliloquies must, I think, be seen as part of Iago's 'honesty'; he is quite open to his own motives or preferences and interested to find out what they are.

The clear cases where Iago thinks himself honest are at a good distance from the Restoration use; they bring him into line with the series of sharp unromantic critics like Jacques and Hamlet:

For I am nothing if not critical

he tells Desdemona to amuse her; his faults, he tells Othello, are due to an excess of this truthful virtue –

I confess, it is my nature's plague
To spy into abuses, and oft my jealousy
Shapes faults that are not.

There seems no doubt that he believes this and thinks it creditable, whatever policy made him say it here; indeed we know it is true from the soliloquies. Now this kind of man is really very unlike the Restoration 'honest fellow', and for myself I find it hard to combine them in one feeling about the word. But in a great deal of Iago's talk to Roderigo – 'drown thyself! drown cats and blind puppies . . . why, thou silly gentleman, I will never love thee after' – he is a wise uncle, obviously honest in the cheerful sense, and for some time this is our main impression of him.* It is still strong during the business of making Cassio drunk; there is no reason

*** It is a very bold and strange irony to make Othello repeat the phrase 'love thee after' just before he kills Desdemona.**

why he should praise the English for their powers of drinking except to make sure that the groundlings are still on his side.

Perhaps the main connection between the two sorts of honest men is not being indulgent towards romantic love:

OTH.: *I cannot speak enough of this content,*
It stops me here; it is too much of joy.
And this, and this, the greatest discords be
That e'er our hearts shall make. (Kissing her).
IAGO: *Oh you are well tun'd now;*
But I'll set down the peggs that make this Musick,
As honest as I am.

The grammar may read 'because I am so honest' as well as 'though I am so honest' and the irony may deny any resultant sense. He is ironical about the suggestions in the patronizing use, which he thinks are applied to him – 'low-class, and stupid, but good-natured'. But he feels himself really 'honest' as the kind of man who can see through nonsense; Othello's affair is a passing lust which has become a nuisance, and Iago can get it out of the way.

It may well be objected that this is far too mild a picture of Iago's plot, and indeed he himself is clearly impressed by its wickedness; at the end of the first act he calls it a 'monstrous birth' and invokes Hell to assist it. But after this handsome theatrical effect the second act begins placidly, in a long scene which includes the 'As honest as I am' passage, and at the end of this scene we find that Iago still imagines he will only

Make the Moor thank me, love me, and reward me
For making him egregiously an ass

– to be sure, the next lines say he will practise on Othello 'even to madness', but even this can be fitted into the picture of the clown who makes 'fools' of other people; it certainly does not envisage the holocaust of the end of the play. Thinking in terms of character, it is clear that Iago has not yet decided how far he will go.

The suggestion of 'stupid' in a patronizing use of *honest* (still clear in 'honest Thompson, my gardener', a Victorian if not a present-day use) brings it near to *fool*; there is a chance for these two rich words to overlap. There is an aspect of Iago in which he is the Restoration 'honest fellow', who is good company because he blows the gaff; but much the clearest example of it is in the beginning of the second act, when he is making sport for his betters. While Desdemona is waiting for Othello's ship, which may have been lost in the tempest, he puts on an elaborate piece of clowning to distract her; and she takes his real opinion of love and women for a piece of hearty and good-natured fun. Iago's kind of honesty, he feels, is not valued as it should be; there is much in Iago of the Clown in Revolt, and the inevitable clown is almost washed out in this play to give him a free field. It is not, I think, dangerously far-fetched to take almost all Shakespeare's uses of *fool* as metaphors from the clown, whose symbolism certainly rode his imagination and was explained to the audience in most of his early plays. Now Iago's defence when Othello at last turns on him, among the rich ironies of its claim to honesty, brings in both *Fool* and the Vice used in *Hamlet* as an old name for the clown.

IAGO: *O wretched fool,*
*That lov'st to make thine Honesty, a Vice!**
Oh monstrous world! Take note, take note (O World)
To be direct and honest is not safe
I thank you for this profit, and from hence
I'll love no Friend, sith Love breeds such offence.
OTH.: *Nay stay; thou should'st be honest.*

* 'And make thyself a motley to the view': Sonnet CX.

IAGO: *I should be wise; for Honesty's a Fool,*
And loses that it works for.
OTH.: *By the world,*
I think my wife be honest, and think she is not.

What comes out here is Iago's unwillingness to be the Fool he thinks he is taken for; but it is dramatic irony as well, and that comes back to his notion of *honest*; he is fooled by the way his plans run away with him; he fails in knowledge of others and perhaps even of his own desires.

Othello swears *by the world* because what Iago has said about being honest in the world, suggesting what worldly people think, is what has made him doubtful; yet the senses of *honest* are quite different – chastity and truth-telling. Desdemona is called a supersubtle Venetian, and he may suspect she would agree with what Iago treats as worldly wisdom; whereas it was her simplicity that made her helpless; though again, the fatal step was her lie about the handkerchief: *Lov'st* in the second line (Folios) seems to me better than *liv'st* (Quarto), as making the frightened Iago bring in his main claim at once; the comma after *Honesty* perhaps makes the sense 'loves with the effect of making' rather than 'delights in making'; in any case *love* appears a few lines down. *Breeds* could suggest sexual love, as if Iago's contempt for that has spread to his notions of friendship; Othello's marriage is what has spoilt their relations (Cassio 'came a-wooing with' Othello, as a social figure, and then got the lieutenantship). In the same way Othello's two uses of *honest* here jump from 'loving towards friends, which breeds honour' to (of women) 'chaste'. It is important I think that the feminine sense, which a later time felt to be quite distinct, is so deeply confused here with the other ones.

It is not safe to be *direct* either way, to be *honest* in Othello's sense or Iago's. The sanctimonious metaphor *profit* might carry satire from Iago on Puritans or show Iago to be like them. Iago is still telling a good deal of truth; the reasons he gives have always made him despise those who are faithful to their masters, if not to their friends. It is clear that he would think himself a bad friend to his real friends. He believes there is a gaff to blow about the ideal love affair, though his evidence has had to be forced. Of course he is using *honest* less in his own way than to impose on Othello, yet there is a real element of self-pity in his complaint. It is no white-washing of Iago – you may hate him the more for it – but he feels he is now in danger because he has gone the 'direct' way to work, exposed false pretensions, and tried to be 'frank' to himself about the whole situation. I do not think this is an oversubtle treatment of his words; behind his fear he is gloating over his cleverness, and seems to delight in the audience provided by the stage.

In the nightmare scene where Othello clings to the word to justify himself he comes near accepting Iago's use of it.

> EMIL.: *My husband!*
> OTH.: *Ay, twas he that told me first:*
> *An honest man he is, and hates the slime*
> *That sticks on filthy deeds . . . .*
> EMIL.: *My husband say that she was false?*
> OTH.: *He, woman;*
> *I say thy husband: dost understand the word?*
> *My friend, thy husband, honest, honest Iago.*

From the sound of the last line it seems as bitter and concentrated as the previous question; to the audience it is. Yet Othello means no irony against Iago, and it is hard to invent a reason for his repetition of *honest*. He may feel it painful that the coarse Iago, not Desdemona or Cassio, should be the only honest creature, or Iago's honesty may suggest the truth he told; or indeed you may call it a trick on the audience, to wind up the irony to its highest before Iago is exposed. Yet Iago would agree that one reason why he was honest was that he hated the slime. The same slime would be produced, by Desdemona as well as by Othello one would hope, if the act of love were of the most rigidly faithful character; the disgust in the metaphor is disgust at all sexuality. Iago playing 'honest' as prude is the rat who stands up for the ideal; as soon as Othello agrees he is finely cheated; Iago is left with his pleasures and Othello's happiness is destroyed. Iago has always despised his pleasures, always treated sex without fuss, like the lavatory; it is by this that he manages to combine the 'honest dog' tone with honesty as Puritanism. The twist of the irony here is that Othello now feels humbled before such clarity. It is a purity he has failed to attain, and he accepts it as a form of honour. The hearty use and the horror of it are united in this appalling line.

Soon after there is a final use of *fool,* by Emilia, which sums up the clown aspect of Iago, but I ought to recognise that it may refer to Othello as well:

EMIL.: *He begged of me to steal it.*
IAGO: *Villainous whore!*
EMIL.: *She give it Cassio! no, alas; I found it,*
And I did give't my husband.
IAGO: *Filth, thou liest!*
EMIL.: *By heaven, I do not, I do not, gentlemen.*
O murderous coxcomb, what should such a fool
Do with so good a wife?
(Iago stabs Emilia and escapes).

On the face of it she praises herself to rebut his insults, which are given because she is not a 'good wife' in the sense of loyal to his interests. But her previous speech takes for granted that 'she' means Desdemona, and we go straight on to Emilia's death-scene, which is entirely selfless and praises Desdemona only. I think she is meant to turn and upbraid Othello, so that she praises Desdemona in this sentence: it would be a convenience in acting, as it explains why she does not notice Iago's sword. *Coxcomb* in any case insists on the full meaning of 'fool', which would make a startling insult for Othello; the idea becomes not that he was stupid to be deceived (a reasonable complaint) but that he was vain of his clownish authority, that is, self-important about his position as a husband and his suspicions, murderous merely because he wanted to show what he could do, like a child. She is the mouthpiece of all the feelings in us which are simply angry with Othello, but this judgement of him is not meant to keep its prominence for long. Indeed as her death-scene goes on the interpretation which the producer should reject is I think meant to come back into our minds; the real murderous coxcomb, the clown who did kill merely out of vanity, was Iago. The cynic had always hated to be treated as a harmless joker, and what finally roused him into stabbing her was perhaps that he thought she had called him a clown. The Lion and the Fox are thus united in the word, but as so many things happen in the play by a misunderstanding. It is perhaps an unnecessarily elaborate interpretation (the reference to Iago is much the more important one) but I think it is needed for our feelings about Emilia that she should not deliberately give herself the praise which we none the less come to feel she deserves.

Some other words which combine the ideas of truth-telling and generosity are affected by the same process as *honest,* though without becoming so important. Desdemona while giggling at the jokes of Iago in the second Act says, 'Is he not a most profane and liberal counsellor?', and Othello echoes this *liberal* when he catches from Iago the trick of sneering at the generosity of Desdemona.

OTH.: *... here's a young and sweating devil here*
That commonly rebels. Tis a good hand,
A frank *one.*
DES.: *You may indeed say so,*
For twas that hand that gave away my heart.
OTH.: *A* liberal *hand ....*

EMILIA: *No, I will speak as* liberal *as the air*
Let heaven and men, and devils, let them all
All, all, cry shame against me, yet I'll speak . . .
So speaking as I think, *I die, I die.*

Indeed the whole power of Emilia's death-scene is that she ties up a variety of sacrificial virtues into a bundle labelled 'mere coarse frankness'. *Honest* itself seems to have rather minor connections with truth-telling, but the play as a whole is far from indifferent to that virtue, and Emilia has to steal the limelight from Iago in the eyes of those who preferred a character who could blow the gaff.

The only later use of *honest* comes when Othello's sword is taken from him by the State officer; a mark of disgrace, a symbol of cuckoldry; two possible negations of honour and honesty.

OTH.: *I am not valiant neither,*
But every puny whisper gets my sword.
But why should honour outlive honesty?
Let it go all.

The straightforward meaning, I take it (though commentators have disagreed a good deal), is something like 'I have lost my civilian reputation, because the killing of my wife has turned out unjust; why then should I care about my military reputation, which depends on keeping my sword?' But the poetic or dramatic effect clearly means a great deal more. The question indeed so sums up the play that it involves nearly all of both words; it seems finally to shatter the concept of honesty whose connecting links the play has patiently removed. There are thirteen other uses of *honour* (and *honourable*); four of them by Othello about himself and five by others about Othello.* The

* The remaining four can all I think be connected with Othello. His wife's honour concerns him directly – the compari-

effect has been to make Othello the personification of honour; if honour does not survive some test of the idea nor could Othello. And to him *honest* is 'honourable', from which it was derived; a test of one is a test of the other. Outlive Desdemona's chastity, which he now admits, outlive Desdemona herself, the personification of chastity (lying again, as he insisted, with her last breath), outlive decent behaviour in, public respect for, self-respect in, Othello – all these are honour, not honesty; there is no question whether Othello outlives them. But they are not tests of an idea; what has been tested is a special sense of *honest*. Iago has been the personification of honesty, not merely to Othello but to his world; why should honour, the father of the word, live on and talk about itself; honesty, that obscure bundle of assumptions, the play has destroyed. I can see no other way to explain the force of the question here.

There is very little for anybody to add to A. C. Bradley's magnificent analysis, but one can maintain that Shakespeare, and the audience he had, and the audience he wanted, saw the thing in rather different proportions. Many of the audience were old soldiers disbanded without pension; they would dislike Cassio

---

son of it to the handkerchief even implies that he has given it to her (IV i 14); Cassio, we hear, is to have an honourable position – because he is to take Othello's place (IV iii 240); the state officer is 'your honour' because he represents the source of that position. The only difficult case is

> *Three lads of Cyprus – noble swelling spirits*
> *That hold their honours in a wary distance . . .*
> *Have I this night flustered with flowing cups* (II iii 53)

It will be hard for Cassio not to get drunk with them because they are 'tough'; their boastful virility is likely to make them dangerous customers unless they are handled on their own footing. I think they act as a faint parody of Othello's Honour, which is a much idealised version of the same kind of thing. And on the other hand Iago does not use the word at all when he is making contradictory speeches in favour of 'good name' and against 'reputation', because that would make it less specific.

as the new type of officer, the boy who can displace men of experience merely because he knows enough mathematics to work the new guns. The tragedy plays into their hands by making Cassio a young fool who can't keep his mistress from causing scandals and can't drink. I don't know why Shakespeare wanted to tell us that Iago was exactly twenty-eight, but anyway he is experienced and Cassio seems about six years younger. Iago gets a long start at the beginning of the play, where he is enchantingly amusing and may be in the right. I am not trying to deny that by the end of the first Act he is obviously the villain, and that by the end of the play we are meant to feel the mystery of his life as Othello did:

Will you, I pray, demand that semi- devil
Why he hath thus ensnared my soul and body?

Shakespeare can now speak his mind about Iago through the convention of the final speech by the highest in rank:

O Spartan dog,
More fell than anguish, hunger, or the sea!

Verbal analysis is not going to weaken the main shape of the thing. But even in this last resounding condemnation the dog is not simple. Dogs come in six times. Roderigo when dying also calls his murderer Iago a dog, and Othello does it conditionally, if Iago prove false. Roderigo says that he himself 'is not like a hound that hunts but one that fills up the cry' – Iago is the dog that hunts, we are to reflect.* Iago says that Cassio when drunk will be 'as full of quarrel and offence as my young mistress's dog'; now Iago himself clearly knows what it feels like to be ready to take offence, and one

* Mr Granville-Barker indeed said that Iago was 'like a hound on the trail, sensitive and alert, nose to the ground, searching and sampling, appetite and instinct combining to guide him past error after error to his quarry'.

might think that this phrase helps to define the sort of dog he is, the spoiled favourite of his betters. He has also a trivial reference to dogs when encouraging Cassio and saying that Othello only pretends to be angry with him 'as one would beat his offenceless dog, to affright an imperious lion.' It seems rather dragged in, as if Iago was to mention dogs as much as possible. The typical Shakespearean dog-men are Apemantus and Thersites (called 'dog' by Homer), malign underdogs, snarling critics, who yet are satisfactory as clowns and carry something of the claim of the disappointed idealist; on the other hand, if there is an obscure prophecy in the treatment of *honest,* surely the 'honest *dog*' of the Restoration may cast something of his shadow before. Wyndham Lewis' interesting treatment of Iago as 'fox' (in *The Lion and the Fox*) leaves out both these dogs, though the dog is more relevant than the fox on his analogy of tragedy to bull-baiting; indeed the clash of the two dogs goes to the root of Iago. But the dog symbolism is a mere incident, like that of *fool;* the thought is carried on *honest,* and I throw in the others only not to over-simplify the thing. Nor are they used to keep Iago from being a straightforward villain; the point is that more force was needed to make Shakespeare's audience hate Iago than to make them accept the obviously intolerable Macbeth as a tragic hero.

There seems a linguistic difference between what Shakespeare meant by Iago and what the nineteenth-century critics saw in him. They took him as an abstract term 'Evil'; he is a critique on an unconscious pun. This is seen more clearly in their own personifications of their abstract word; e.g. *The Turn of the Screw* and *Dr Jekyll and Mr Hyde.* Henry James got a great triumph over some critic who said that his villains were sexual perverts (if the story meant anything they could hardly be anything else). He said: 'Ah, you have been letting yourself have fancies about Evil; I kept it right out of my mind.' That indeed is what the story is about. Stevenson rightly made clear that *Dr*

Jekyll is about hypocrisy. You can only consider Evil as all things that destroy the good life; this has no unity; for instance, Hyde could not be both the miser and the spendthrift and whichever he was would destroy Jekyll without further accident. Evil here is merely the daydream of a respectable man, and only left vague so that respectable readers may equate it unshocked to their own daydreams. Iago may not be a 'personality', but he is better than these; he is the product of a more actual interest in a word.

II

It struck me on reading this over that it is not likely to convince a supporter of Bradley, since it bows to the master as if taking his results for granted and then appears to include him among the nineteenth-century critics who are denounced; also, what is more important, it does not answer the central question that Bradley put – 'Why does Iago plot at all?' I shall try now to summarize Bradley's position and explain the points at which I disagree from it.

We are shown, says Bradley, that Iago is clear-sighted, and he appears to have been prudent till the play begins; he must have realized that his plot was extremely dangerous to himself (in the event it was fatal); and yet we feel that he is not actuated by any passion of hatred or ambition – in fact, so far as he pretends that he is, he seems to be wondering what his motives for action can be, almost as Hamlet (in the immediately previous play by Shakespeare) wonders what his motives can be for inaction.* Some recent critics have objected to this sort of analysis, but I think it is clearly wrong to talk as if coherence of character is not needed in poetic drama, only coherence of metaphor and so on. The fair

* One might indeed claim that Iago is a satire on the holy thought of Polonius – 'To thine own self be true . . . thou canst not then be false to any man.'

point to make against Bradley's approach (as is now generally agreed) is that the character of Iago must have been intended to seem coherent to the first-night audience; therefore the solution cannot be reached by learned deductions from hints in the text about his previous biography, for instance; if the character is puzzling nowadays, the answer must be a matter of recalling the assumptions of the audience and the way the character was put across. Of course it is also possible that Shakespeare was cheating, and that the audience would not care as long as they got their melodrama. Indeed there are lines in Iago's soliloquies which seem to be using the older convention, by which the villain merely announced his villainy in terms such as the good people would have used about him. But I should maintain that the character was an eminently interesting one to the first-night audience (they did not take the villain for granted) and that even the crudities could be absorbed into a realistic view of him. Such at any rate is the question at issue.

Bradley's answer is in brief that Iago is tempted by vanity and love of plotting. Iago says he likes 'to plume up his will/In double knavery', to heighten his sense of power by plots, and Bradley rightly points out that this reassurance to the sense of power is a common reason for apparently meaningless petty cruelties. Iago particularly wants to do it at this time, because he has been slighted by Cassio's appointment and is in irritating difficulties with Roderigo, so that 'his thwarted sense of superiority demands satisfaction'. But he knows at the back of his mind that his plot is dangerous to the point of folly, and that is why he keeps inventing excuses for himself. Bradley opposes what seems to have been a common Victorian view that Iago had 'a general disinterested love of evil', and says that if he had a 'motiveless malignity' (Coleridge) it was only in the more narrow but more psychologically plausible way that Bradley has defined.

All this I think is true, and satisfies the condition about the first-night audience. The thwarted sense of superiority in Iago is thrust on them in the first scene, and they are expected to feel a good deal of sympathy for it; at the end of the first Act they are to appreciate the triumph with which he conceives the plot. However the question 'why does he do it?' would hardly present itself as a problem; obviously the play required a villain; the only question likely to arise is 'why does everybody take the villain for a good man?' Bradley of course recognises this question but he deals with it in terms of an ethical theory supposed to be held only by Iago, whereas you clearly need to consider how it was understood by the audience; and the effect of this twist is to take Bradley some way back towards the idea that Iago embodies Pure Evil.

He says that Iago has 'a spite against goodness in men as a thing not only stupid but, both in its nature and by its success, contrary to Iago's nature and irritating to his pride'. Not only that, but 'His creed – for he is no sceptic, he has a definite creed – is that absolute egoism is the only rational and proper attitude, and that conscience or honour or any kind of regard for others is an absurdity.' Bradley therefore finds it contradictory and somewhat pathetic when Iago shouts 'villainous whore' at his wife, or implies that since Cassio would like to be an adulterer it is not so bad to say he is one (III i 311). This, he says, shows that Iago has a 'secret subjection to morality', an 'inability to live up to his creed'; also the soliloquies betray a desire to convince himself, so that his natural egoism is not perfect. Perfection is attained, however, in the way he hides his ethical theory from other people; when we consider his past life, says Bradley, 'the inference, which is accompanied by a thrill of admiration, (is) that Iago's power of dissimulation and of self-control must have been prodigious'. Since a thrill about his past life is not properly part of the play, this amounts to an admission that the stage character is not consistent. In effect, Bradley is agreeing with Rymer here.

It seems clear that Iago was not meant as a secret theoretician of this sort, and that the audience would not be misled into thinking him one. His opinions, so far as he has got them clear, are shared by many people around him, and he boasts about them freely. To be sure, he could not afford to do this if they were not very confused, but even the confusion is shared by his neighbours. When Iago expounds his egotism to Roderigo, in the first scene of the play, he is not so much admitting a weak criminal to his secrets as making his usual claim to Sturdy Independence in a rather coarser form. He is not subservient to the interests of the men in power who employ him, he says; he can stand up for himself, as they do. No doubt an Elizabethan employer, no less than Professor Bradley, would think this a shocking sentiment; but it does not involve Pure Egotism, and I do not even see that it involves Machiavelli. It has the air of a spontaneous line of sentiment among the lower classes, whereas Machiavelli was interested in the deceptions necessary for a ruler. Certainly it does not imply that the Independent man will betray his friends (as apart from his employer), because if it did he would not boast about it to them. This of course is the answer to the critics who have said that Roderigo could not have gone on handing all his money to a self-confessed knave. And, in the same way, when it turns out that Iago does mean to betray Roderigo, he has only to tell the audience that this fool is not one of his real friends; indeed he goes on to claim that it would be *wrong* to treat him as one. I do not mean to deny there is a paradox about the whole cult of the Independent Man (it is somehow felt that his selfishness makes him more valuable as a friend); but the paradox was already floating in the minds of the audience. No doubt Shakespeare thought that the conception was a false one, and gave a resounding demonstration of it, but one need not suppose that he did this by inventing a unique psychology for Iago, or even by making Iago unusually conscious of the problem at issue.

Indeed, when Iago is a conscious hypocrite, I should have thought that he was laughably unconvincing:

Though in the trade of war I have slain men,
Yet I do hold it very stuff of the conscience
To do no contrived murder: I lack iniquity
Sometimes to do me service; nine or ten times
I thought to have yerked him here under the ribs.

''Tis better as it is', answers Othello rather shortly; they are his first words in the play. Iago's attempt to show fine feelings has only made him sound like a ruffian in Marlowe. But this is not at all likely to shake Othello's faith in him; the idea is that, if you are in the way of needing a reliable bodyguard, you must put up with something rough. It is true that the soliloquies make him seem a more intellectual type; and when he says, as a reason for murdering Cassio, 'He has a daily beauty in his life, Which makes me ugly', one can hardly deny that Shakespeare is making a crude use of the soliloquy convention. But even this line, though false, is only so in a marginal way. We feel that Iago would not have used those words, but Shakespeare is already committed to the convention of making him talk poetry. The trouble is that the phrase seems to refer to the *moral* beauty of Cassio, on which Bradley expresses some delicate thoughts, and indeed this line is probably what made Bradley believe that Iago has both a clear recognition of goodness and a positive spite against it.* But it is plausible enough (as a 'second level' interpretation of the crude convention) to say that Iago only means that Cassio has smarter clothes and more upper-class manners, which give him an unfair advantage over Iago (for one thing, that is why Iago fears Cassio with his nightcap). The resentment of the

* Mr Wilson Knight, in 'The *Othello* Music', also regards the 'daily beauty' speech as the essence of the matter; in the same way, he says, Iago hates the romance of Othello and the purity of Desdemona, and 'this is his "motive" throughout; other suggestions are surface deep only'. No doubt he is drawn as a cynic, but I do not think the audience would take cynicism as such to be something purely devilish and consciously devoted to destroying goodness or beauty in any form; because the cynic had a claim to be a Puritan.

lower classes towards the graces of the upper really has been known to take ugly forms, and Shakespeare with his new coat of arms was ready to go out of his way to reprove it. The phrase comes late in the play (early in the fifth Act) where Iago can in any case be treated simply as the villain; it is assumed that the feeling of the audience has been swung firmly against him. Mr Granville-Barker said that it is a 'strange involuntary phrase' which Iago 'quickly obliterates under more matter-of-fact language'; and marks the point where 'even his nerve is strained', so that he is beginning to bungle a situation which has got more complicated than he meant (he has obviously got to kill Cassio anyhow). This seems to me an excellent tip for a modern actor but not necessarily part of the first idea.

As to the puzzle about why he is not suspected, he boasts of that too, in a prominent place, at the end of a soliloquy and a scene (II i).

Knavery's plain face is never seen, till us'd.

Shakespeare here outfaces the difficulty by a challenge to the audience: 'You would have been fooled too, though you may think you wouldn't.' And the reason seems clear enough from the preceding soliloquy, though it is not what Iago meant to say. His accumulating resentments at his inferior position have become explosive, so that he imagines slights from every direction; but people cannot expect this because it seems to them natural that his position should be inferior. And yet (says the line) his knavery has always had a 'plain face' – his jeering wit and his sturdy independence had always been his stock-in-trade.

I have gone into the matter at perhaps tedious length without using the word *honest* at all, because there seems a suggestion of trickery or triviality about saying that the character is only made plausible by puns on one word. Perhaps this is a risky manoeuvre, because the more I succeeded in it the harder it would become to claim that the puns on *honest* were essential to the play. But it is clear I think that all the elements of the character are represented in the range of meanings of *honest*, and (what is more important) that the confusion of moral theory in the audience, which would make them begin by approving of Iago (though perhaps only in the mixed form of the 'ironical cheer'), was symbolised or echoed in a high degree by the confusion of the word. When opinion had become more settled or conventionalised, and the word had itself followed this movement by becoming simpler, there were of course two grounds for finding a puzzle in the character; but, of the two, I should say that failure to appreciate the complexity of the word was the more important ground, because after all the complexity of moral judgement had not become so difficult – what people had lost was the verbal pointer directing them to it. I think indeed that the Victorians were not ready enough to approve the good qualities of being 'ready to blow the gaff' and 'frank to yourself about your own desires'; and it is not likely that any analysis of one word would have altered their opinions. And I must admit (as a final effort to get the verbalist approach into its right proportion) that my opinions about the play date from seeing an actual performance of it, with a particularly good Iago, and that I did not at the time think about the word *honest* at all. The verbal analysis came when I looked at the text to see what support it gave to these impressions. But I do not feel this to be any reason for doubting that the puns on *honesty* really do support them.

SOURCE: *The Structure of Complex Words* (1951).

F. R. Leavis

DIABOLIC INTELLECT AND THE NOBLE HERO (1952)

Othello, it will be very generally granted, is of all Shakespeare's great tragedies the simplest: the theme is limited and sharply defined, and the play, everyone agrees, is a brilliantly successful piece of workmanship. The effect is one of a noble, 'classical' clarity – of firm, clear outlines, unblurred and undistracted by cloudy recessions, metaphysical aura, or richly symbolical ambiguities.[1] There would, it seems, be something like a consensus in this sense. And yet it is of *Othello* that one can say bluntly, as of no other of the great tragedies, that it suffers in current appreciation an essential and denaturing falsification.

The generally recognized peculiarity of *Othello* among the tragedies may be indicated by saying that it lends itself as no other of them does to the approach classically associated with Bradley's name: even *Othello* (it will be necessary to insist) is poetic drama, a dramatic poem, and not a psychological novel written in dramatic form and draped in poetry, but relevant discussion of its tragic significance will nevertheless be mainly a matter of character-analysis. It would, that is, have lent itself uniquely well to Bradley's approach if Bradley had made his approach consistently and with moderate intelligence. Actually, however, the section on *Othello* in *Shakespearean Tragedy* is more extravagant in misdirected scrupulosity than any of the others; it is, with a concentration of Bradley's comical solemnity, completely wrong-headed – grossly and palpably false to the evidence it offers to weigh. Grossly and palpably? – yet Bradley's *Othello* is substantially that of common acceptance. And here is the reason for dealing with it, even though not only Bradley but, in its turn, disrespect for Bradley (one gathers) has gone out of fashion (as a matter of fact he is still a very potent and mischievous influence).

According to the version of *Othello* elaborated by Bradley the tragedy is the undoing of the noble Moor by the devilish cunning of Iago. Othello we are to see as a nearly faultless hero whose strength and virtue are turned against him. Othello and Desdemona, so far as their fate depended on their characters and untampered-with mutual relations, had every ground for expecting the happiness that romantic courtship had promised. It was external evil, the malice of the demi-devil, that turned a happy story of romantic love – of romantic lovers who were qualified to live happily ever after, so to speak – into a tragedy. This – it is the traditional version of *Othello* and has, moreover, the support of Coleridge – is to sentimentalize Shakespeare's tragedy and to displace its centre.

Here is Bradley:

> Turning from the hero and the heroine to the third principal character we observe (what has often been pointed out) that the action and catastrophe of *Othello* depend largely on intrigue. We must not say more than this. We must not call the play a tragedy of intrigue as distinguished from a tragedy of character. (p. 179)

And we must not suppose that Bradley sees what is in front of him. The character he is thinking of isn't Othello's. 'Iago's plot', he goes on.

> Iago's plot is Iago's character in action.

In fact the play (we need hardly stop short of saying) is Iago's character in action. Bradley adds, it is true, that Iago's plot 'is built on his knowledge of Othello's character, and could not otherwise have succeeded'. But Iago's knowledge of Othello's character amounts pretty much to Bradley's knowledge of it (except, of course, that Iago cannot realize Othello's nobility quite to the full): Othello is purely noble, strong, generous, and trusting, and as tragic hero is, however formidable and destructive in his agonies, merely a victim – the victim of Iago's devilish 'intellectual superiority' (which is 'so great that we watch its advance fascinated and appalled'). It is all in order, then, that Iago should get one of the two lectures that Bradley gives to the play, Othello sharing the other with Desdemona. And it is all in the tradition; from Coleridge down, Iago – his motivation or his motivelessness – has commonly been, in commentaries on the play, the main focus of attention.

The plain fact that has to be asserted in the face of this sustained and sanctioned perversity is that in Shakespeare's tragedy of *Othello* Othello is the chief personage – the chief personage in such a sense that the tragedy may fairly be said to be Othello's character in action. Iago is subordinate and merely ancillary. He is not much more than a necessary piece of dramatic mechanism – that at any rate is a fit reply to the view of Othello as necessary material and provocation for a display of Iago's fiendish intellectual superiority. Iago, of course, is sufficiently convincing as a person; he could not perform his dramatic function otherwise. But something has gone wrong when we make him interesting in this kind of way:

> His fate – which is himself – has completely mastered him: so that, in the later scenes, where the improbability of the entire success of a design built on so many different falsehoods forces itself on the reader, Iago appears for moments not as a consummate schemer, but as a man absolutely infatuated and delivered over to certain destruction.

We ought not, in reading those scenes, to be paying so much attention to the intrinsic personal qualities of Iago as to attribute to him tragic interest of that kind.

This last proposition, though its justice is perhaps

not self-evident, must remain for the time being a matter of assertion. Other things come first. Othello has in any case the prior claim on our attention, and it seems tactically best to start with something as easy to deal with as the view – Bradley's and Coleridge's[2] – and of course, Othello's before them – that Othello was 'not easily jealous'. Easy to deal with because there, to point to, is the text, plain and unequivocal. And yet the text was there for Coleridge, and Bradley accompanies his argument with constant particular reference to it. It is as extraordinary a history of triumphant sentimental perversity as literary history can show. Bradley himself saves us the need of insisting on this diagnosis by carrying indulgence of his preconception, his determined sentimental preconception, to such heroic lengths:

> Now I repeat that *any* man situated as Othello was would have been disturbed by Iago's communications, and I add that many men would have been made wildly jealous. But up to this point, where Iago is dismissed [III iii 238], Othello, I must maintain, does not show jealousy. His confidence is shaken, he is confused and deeply troubled, he feels even horror; but he is not yet jealous in the proper sense of that word.

The 'proper sense of that word' is perhaps illustrated by these lines (not quoted by Bradley) in which, Bradley grants, 'the beginning of that passion may be traced':

> Haply, for I am black
> And have not those soft parts of conversation
> That chamberers have, or for I am declined
> Into the vale of years – yet that's not much –
> She's gone; I am abused, and my relief
> Must be to loathe her. O curse of marriage,
> That we can call these delicate creatures ours,
> And not their appetites! I had rather be a toad,

And live upon the vapour of a dungeon,
Than keep a corner in the thing I love
For others' uses.

Any reader not protected by a very obstinate preconception would take this, not for a new development of feeling, but for the fully explicit expression of something he had already, pages back, registered as an essential element in Othello's behaviour – something the evoking of which was essential to Iago's success. In any case, jealous or not jealous 'in the proper sense of that word', Othello has from the beginning responded to Iago's communications' in the way Iago desired and with a promptness that couldn't be improved upon, and has dismissed Iago with these words:

Farewell, farewell:
If more thou dost perceive, let me know more;
Set on thy wife to observe,

to observe Desdemona, concerning whom Iago has just said:

Ay, there's the point: as – to be bold with you –
Not to affect many proposed matches
Of her own clime, complexion and degree,
Whereto we see in all things nature tends –
Foh! one may smell in such a will most rank,
Foul disproportion, thoughts unnatural.
But pardon me: I do not in position
Distinctly speak of her, though I may fear
Her will, recoiling to her better judgment,
May fall to match you with her country forms,
And happily repent.

To say that it's not jealousy here is hardly (one would have thought) to bring Othello off clean; but Bradley's conclusion is not (as might have seemed inevitable) that there may be other faults than jealousy that are at least as damaging to a man in the character of husband and married lover. He is quite explicit:

> Up to this point, it seems to me, there is not a syllable to be said against Othello. (p. 194)

With such resolute fidelity does Bradley wear these blinkers that he can say,

> His trust, where he trusts, is absolute,

without realizing the force of the corollary: Othello's trust, then, can never have been in Desdemona. It is the vindication of Othello's perfect nobility that Bradley is preoccupied with, and we are to see the immediate surrender to Iago as part of that nobility. But to make absolute trust in Iago – trust at Desdemona's expense – a manifestation of perfect nobility is (even if we ignore what it makes of Desdemona) to make Iago a very remarkable person indeed. And that, Bradley, tradition aiding and abetting, proceeds to do.

However, to anyone not wearing these blinkers it is plain that no subtilization and exaltation of the Iago-devil (with consequent subordination of Othello) can save the noble hero of Bradley's devotion. And it is plain that what we should see in Iago's prompt success is not so much Iago's diabolic intellect as Othello's readiness to respond. Iago's power, in fact, in the temptation-scene is that he represents something that is in Othello – in Othello the husband of Desdemona: the essential traitor is within the gates. For if Shakespeare's Othello too is simple-minded, he is nevertheless more complex than Bradley's. Bradley's Othello is, rather, Othello's; it being an essential datum regarding the Shakespearean Othello that he has an ideal conception of himself.

The tragedy is inherent in the Othello–Desdemona relation, and Iago is a mechanism necessary for precipitating tragedy in a dramatic action. Explaining how it should be that Othello, who is so noble and trustful ('Othello, we have seen, was trustful, and thorough in his trust'), can so immediately doubt his wife, Bradley says:

> But he was newly married; in the circumstances he cannot have known much of Desdemona before his marriage. (p. 192)

Again we read:

> But it is not surprising that his utter powerlessness to repel it [Iago's insinuation] on the ground of knowledge of his wife ... should complete his misery.... (p. 193)

Bradley, that is, in his comically innocent way, takes it as part of the datum that Othello really knows nothing about his wife. Ah, but he was in love with her. And so poetically. 'For', says Bradley, 'there is no love, not that of Romeo in his youth, more steeped in imagination than Othello's.' Othello, however, we are obliged to remark (Bradley doesn't make the point in this connection) is not in his youth; he is represented as middle-aged – as having attained at any rate to maturity in that sense. There might seem to be dangers in such a situation, quite apart from any intervention by an Iago. But then, we are told Othello is 'of a great openness and trustfulness of nature'. – It would be putting it more to the point to say that he has great consciousness of worth and confidence of respect.

The worth is really and solidly there; he is truly impressive, a noble product of the life of action – of

> The big wars
> That make ambition virtue.

'That make ambition virtue' – this phrase of his is a key one: his virtues are, in general, of that kind; they have, characteristically, something of the quality suggested. Othello, in his magnanimous way, is egotistic.

He really is, beyond any question, the nobly massive man of action, the captain of men, he sees himself as being, but he does very much see himself:

> Keep up your bright swords, for the dew will rust them.

In short, a habit of self-approving self-dramatization is an essential element in Othello's make-up, and remains so at the very end.

It is, at the best, the impressive manifestation of a noble egotism. But, in the new marital situation, this egotism isn't going to be the less dangerous for its nobility. This self-centredness doesn't mean self-knowledge: that is a virtue which Othello, as soldier of fortune, hasn't had much need of. He has been well provided by nature to meet all the trials a life of action has exposed him to. The trials facing him now that he has married this Venetian girl with whom he's 'in love' so imaginatively (we're told) as to outdo Romeo and who is so many years younger than himself (his colour, whether or not 'colour-feeling' existed among the Elizabethans, we are certainly to take as emphasizing the disparity of the match) – the trials facing him now are of a different order.

And here we have the significance of the storm, which puts so great a distance between Venice and Cyprus, between the old life and the new, and makes the change seem so complete and so momentous. The storm is rendered in that characteristic heroic mode of the play which Professor Wilson Knight[3] calls the '*Othello* music':

> For do but stand upon the foaming shore,
> The chidden billows seem to chide the clouds;
> The wind-shaked surge, with high and monstrous mane,
> Seems to cast water on the burning bear,
> And quench the guards of the ever-fixed pole:
> I never did like molestation view
> On the enchafed flood. (II i)

This mode (Professor Wilson Knight, in his own way, describes it well) gives the effect of a comparatively simple magnificence; the characteristic verse of *Othello* is firm, regular in outline, buoyant and sonorous. It is in an important sense Othello's own verse, the 'large-mouthed utterance' of the noble man of action. Bradley's way of putting it is that Othello, though he 'has not, indeed, the meditative or speculative imagination of Hamlet', is 'in the strictest sense of the word' 'more poetic than Hamlet' (p 188). We need not ask Bradley what the 'strictest sense of the word' is, or stop to dispute with him whether or not Othello is 'the greatest poet' of all Shakespeare's heroes. If characters in poetic drama speak poetry we ought to be able to notice the fact without concluding that they are poets. In *Othello*, which is poetic drama, Shakespeare works by poetic means: it is through the characteristic noble verse described above that, very largely, we get our sense of the noble Othello. If the impression made by Othello's own utterance is often poetical as well as poetic, that is Shakespeare's way, not of representing him as a poet, but of conveying the romantic glamour that, for Othello himself and others, invests Othello and what he stands for.

'For Othello himself' – it might be said that to express Othello's sense of himself and make us share it is the essential function of this verse, the '*Othello* music'. But, of course, there are distinctions to be noted. The description of the storm quoted above, though it belongs to the general heroic mode of the play, cannot be said to exhibit the element of self-dramatization that is characteristic of Othello's own utterances. On the other hand, the self-dramatizing trick commands subtle modulations and various stops. It is not always as assertive as in

Behold, I have a weapon (v ii 257)

or the closing speech. In these speeches, not only is it explicit, it clearly involves, we may note, an attitude *towards* the emotion expressed – an attitude of a kind we are familiar with in the analysis of sentimentality.

The storm, within the idealizing mode, is at the other extreme from sentimentality; it serves to bring out the reality of the heroic Othello and what he represents. For his heroic quality, realized in this verse (here the utterance of others), is a real thing, though it is not, as Othello takes it to be, the whole of the reality. Another way of making the point would be to say that the distinctive style under discussion, the style that lends itself to Othello's self-dramatization and conveys in general the tone and ideal import of this, goes, in its confident and magnificent buoyancy, essentially with the outer storm that both the lovers, in their voyage to Cyprus, triumphantly outride.

With that kind of external stress the noble Othello is well qualified to deal (if he went down – and we know he won't – he would go down magnificently). But it is not that kind of stress he has to fear in the new life beginning at Cyprus. The stresses of the spiritual climate are concentrated by Iago (with his deflating, unbeglamouring, brutally realistic mode of speech) into something immediately apprehensible in drama and comparable with the storm. In this testing, Othello's inner timbers begin to part at once, the stuff of which he is made begins at once to deteriorate and show itself unfit. There is even a symbolic foundering when, breaking into incoherent ejaculations, he 'falls in a trance' (IV i 35).

As for the justice of this view that Othello yields with extraordinary promptness to suggestion, with such promptness as to make it plain that the mind that undoes him is not Iago's but his own, it does not seem to need arguing. If it has to be argued, the only difficulty is the difficulty, for written criticism, of going in detailed commentary through an extended text. The text is plain enough. Iago's sustained attack begins at about line 90 in Act III, scene iii, immediately upon Desdemona's exit and Othello's exclamation:

Excellent wretch! Perdition catch my soul,
But I do love thee! and when I love thee not,
Chaos is come again.

In seventy lines Othello is brought to such a state that Iago can, without getting any reply but

O misery,

say

O, beware, my lord, of jealousy,

and use the word 'cuckold'. In ninety lines Othello is saying

Why did I marry?

The explanation of this quick work is given plainly enough here:

Iago: I would not have your free and noble nature
Out of self-bounty be abused; look to't:
I know our country disposition well;
In Venice they do let heaven see the pranks
They dare not show their husbands; their best conscience
Is not to leave't undone, but keep't unknown.
Othello: Dost thou say so?
Iago: She did deceive her father, marrying you;
And when she seem'd to shake and fear your looks,
She loved them most.
Othello: And so she did.

There in the first two lines is, explicitly appealed to by Iago,* Othello's ideal conception of himself: it would be a pity if he let it be his undoing (as it actually was – the full irony Iago can hardly be credited with in-

* Who has described Othello (I i 12) as 'loving his own pride and purposes'.

tending). And there in the last line we have the noble and magnanimous Othello, romantic hero and married lover, accepting as evidence against his wife the fact that, at the willing sacrifice of everything else, she had made with him a marriage of romantic love. Iago, like Bradley, points out that Othello didn't really know Desdemona, and Othello acquiesces in considering her as a type – a type outside his experience – the Venetian wife. It is plain, then, that his love is composed very largely of ignorance of self as well as ignorance of her: however nobly he may feel about it, it isn't altogether what he, and Bradley with him, thinks it is. It may be love, but it can be only in an oddly qualified sense love of her: it must be much more a matter of self-centred and self-regarding satisfactions – pride, sensual possessiveness, appetite, love of loving – than he suspects.

This comes out unmistakably when he begins to let himself go; for instance, in the soliloquy that follows Iago's exit:

> She's gone; I am abused, and my relief
> Must be to loathe her. O curse of marriage,
> That we can call these delicate creatures ours,
> And not their appetites! I had rather be a toad,
> And live upon the vapour of a dungeon,
> Than keep a corner in the thing I love
> For others' uses.

Even the actual presence of Desdemona, who enters immediately upon the close of this soliloquy, can avail nothing against the misgivings of angry egotism. Pointing to his forehead he makes an allusion to the cuckold's horns, and when she in her innocence misunderstands him and offers to soothe the pain he rebuffs her. The element of angry sensuality is insistent:

> What sense had I of her stol'n hours of lust?
> ...
> I had been happy if the general camp,
> Pioners and all, had tasted her sweet body.

It is significant that, at the climax of the play, when Othello, having exclaimed

O blood, blood, blood,

kneels to take a formal vow of revenge, he does so in the heroic strain of the '*Othello* music'. To Iago's

Patience, I say; your mind perhaps may change,

he replies:

Never, Iago. Like to the Pontic sea,
Whose icy current and compulsive course
Ne'er feels retiring ebb, but keeps due on
To the Propontic and the Hellespont;
Even so my bloody thoughts, with violent pace,
Shall ne'er look back, ne'er ebb to humble love,
Till that a wide and capable revenge
Swallow them up. Now, by yond marble heaven,
In the due reverence of a sacred vow
I here engage my words.

At this climax of the play, as he sets himself irrevocably in his vindictive resolution, he reassumes formally his heroic self-dramatization – reassumes the Othello of 'the big wars that make ambition virtue'. The part of this conscious nobility, this noble egotism, this self-pride that was justified by experience irrelevant to the present trials and stresses, is thus underlined. Othello's self-idealization, his promptness to jealousy and his blindness are shown in their essential relation. The self-idealization is shown as blindness and the nobility as here no longer something real, but the disguise of an obtuse and brutal egotism. Self-pride becomes stupidity, ferocious stupidity, an insane and self-deceiving passion. The habitual 'nobility' is seen to make self-deception invincible, the egotism it expresses being the drive to catastrophe. Othello's noble lack of self-knowledge is shown as humiliating and disastrous.

Bradley, however, his knowledge of Othello coinciding virtually with Othello's, sees nothing but the nobility. At the cost of denaturing Shakespeare's tragedy, he insistently idealizes. The 'feelings of jealousy proper', he says (p. 194), 'are not the chief or deepest source of Othello's suffering. It is the feeling, "If she be false, oh then Heaven mocks itself;" the feeling, "O Iago, the pity of it, Iago!"' It is Shakespeare's tragedy of Othello that the man who exclaims this can exclaim three lines later, when he next speaks (IV i 204):

> I will chop her into messes. Cuckold me!

Again, three lines further on he says:

> Get me some poison, Iago; this night. I'll not expostulate with her, lest her body and beauty unprovide my mind again: this night, Iago.

This surely has some bearing on the nature of 'the pity of it': to equate Bradley's knowledge of Othello with Othello's own was perhaps unfair to Othello.

In any case, this association of strong sensuality with ugly vindictive jealousy is insistent in Shakespeare's play:

> Now he tells how she plucked him to my chamber. O, I see that nose of yours, but not that dog I shall throw it to. (IV i 140)

> I would have him nine years a-killing. A fine woman! a fair woman! a sweet woman! (IV i 181)

'O Iago, the pity of it, Iago!': it is plain here that 'fine', 'fair' and 'sweet' apply, not to Desdemona as a complete person (the immediate provocation is Iago's remark, 'she gave it him and he hath given it [the handkerchief] his whore'), but to her person in abstraction from the character of the owner, whom Othello hardly, at this point, respects. And the nature of this regret, this tragically expressed regret, bears an essential relation to the nature of the love with which Othello, however imaginatively and Romeo-like, loved Desdemona. That romantic idealizing love could be as dubiously grounded in reality as this is an essential condition of the tragedy. But Bradley's own idealizing is invincible. He can even say (p. 197):

> An ineradicable instinct of justice, rather than any last quiver of hope, leads him to question Emilia.

That's no doubt how Othello would have put it; but for the reader – the unidealizing reader – what the questioning of Emilia (IV ii) shows in brutal, resolute, unrestricted predominance is the antithesis of any instinct of justice.

With obtuseness to the tragic significance of Shakespeare's play goes insensibility to his poetry – to his supreme art as exhibited locally in the verse (it is still not superfluous to insist that the poetic skill is one with the dramatic). This is Bradley's commentary on Act V, scene ii:

> The supposed death of Cassio (V i) satiates the thirst for vengeance. The Othello who enters the bedchamber with the words,
>
> It is the cause, it is the cause, my soul,
>
> is not the man of the Fourth Act. The deed he is bound to do is no murder, but a sacrifice. He is to save Desdemona from herself, not in hate but in honour; in honour, and also in love. His anger has passed; a boundless sorrow has taken its place; and
>
> this sorrow's heavenly:
> It strikes where it doth love.
>
> Even when, at the sight of her apparent obduracy,

> and at the hearing of words which by a crowning fatality can only reconvince him of her guilt, these feelings give way to others, it is to righteous indignation they give way, not to rage: and, terribly painful as this scene is, there is almost nothing here to diminish the admiration and love which heighten pity. (p 197)

That again, no doubt, is how Othello (though as for satiated thirst, he says at line 74,

> Had all his hairs been lives, my great revenge
> Had stomach for them all)

would like to see it. But Bradley, in the speech he quotes from, misses all the shifts of tone by which Shakespeare renders the shifting confusion of Othello's mind. For it is a speech one might have chosen with the express view of illustrating that subtle command of tone which marks Shakespeare's mature art, and which makes the poetry of *Othello* so different in kind from that of *Romeo and Juliet,* and the two dramas consequently incomparable.

It opens with the accent of a contained holy revulsion, the containing power appearing as inexorable, impersonal justice

> It is the cause, it is the cause, my soul!
> Let me not name it to you, you chaste stars!
> It is the cause.

Now comes a shrinking back from the deed:

> Yet I'll not shed her blood,
> Nor scar that whiter skin of hers than snow
> And smooth as monumental alabaster.

Tenderness here quite clearly is that characteristic voluptuousness of Othello's which, since it is unassociated with any real interest in Desdemona as a person, slips so readily into possessive jealousy. Now the accent of impersonal justice is heard again –

> Yet she must die, else she'll betray more men

– but the accent is so clearly unrelated to any effectual motive in Othello that the concern for justice, the self-bracing to noble sacrifice, appears as self-deception. Next come misgivings over the finality of the deed:

> Put out the light, and then put out the light:
> If I quench thee, thou flaming minister,
> I can again thy former light restore,
> Should I repent me: but once put out thy light,
> Thou cunning'st pattern of excelling nature,
> I know not where is that Promethean heat
> That can thy light relume. When I have pluck'd the rose
> I cannot give it vital growth again,
> It must needs wither: I'll smell it on the tree.

Tenderness here is less specifically voluptuous sensuality than it was earlier, but we nevertheless remember:

> Get me some poison, Iago; this night. I'll not expostulate with her, lest her body and beauty unprovide my mind again: this night, Iago.
> (IV i 208)

And there is in Othello a curious and characteristic effect of self-preoccupation, of preoccupation with his emotions rather than with Desdemona in her own right:

> O balmy breath, that almost dost persuade
> Justice to break her sword! One more, one more:
> Be thus when thou art dead, and I will kill thee,
> And love thee after: one more, and this the last.
> So sweet was ne'er so fatal. I must weep,
> But they are cruel tears: this sorrow's heavenly;
> It strikes where it doth love. She wakes.

When she is awake and so is no longer a mere body, but a person, it is not sorrowful love or noble self-bracing to a sacrifice that she becomes aware of in Othello:

> Alas, why gnaw you so your nether lip?
> Some bloody passion shakes your very frame:
> These are portents.

Moreover, though Othello says

> I would not kill thy unprepared spirit,

actually he refuses her the time to say one prayer.

When he discovers his mistake, his reaction is an intolerably intensified form of the common 'I could kick myself':

> Whip me, ye devils
> From the possession of this heavenly sight!
> Blow me about in winds! roast me in sulphr!
> Wash me in steep-down gulfs of liquid fire!
> O Desdemona! Desdemona! dead!
> Oh! Oh! Oh!

But he remains the same Othello; he has discovered his mistake, but there is no tragic self-discovery. The speech closing with the lines just quoted is that beginning

> Behold, I have a weapon,

one of the finest examples in the play of the self-dramatizing trick. The noble Othello is now seen as tragically pathetic, and he sees himself as pathetic too:

> Man but a rush against Othello's breast,
> And he retires. Where shall Othello go?

He is ruined, but he is the same Othello in whose essential make-up the tragedy lay: the tragedy doesn't involve the idea of the hero's learning through suffering. The fact that Othello tends to sentimentalize should be the reverse of a reason for our sentimentalizing too.

For even, or rather especially, in that magnificent last speech of his Othello does tend to sentimentalize,[4] though to say that and no more would convey a false impression, for the speech conveys something like the full complexity of Othello's simple nature, and in the total effect the simplicity is tragic and grand. The quiet beginning gives us the man of action with his habit of effortless authority:

> Soft you; a word or two before you go.
> I have done the State some service, and they know't.
> No more of that. I pray you in your letters,
> When you shall these unlucky deeds relate,
> Speak of me as I am; nothing extenuate,
> Nor set down aught in malice....

Othello really is, we cannot doubt, the stoic-captain whose few words know their full sufficiency: up to this point we cannot say he dramatizes himself, he simply *is*. But then, in a marvellous way (if we consider Shakespeare's art), the emotion works itself up until in less than half-a-dozen lines the stoic of few words is eloquently weeping. With

> Then must you speak
> Of one that loved not wisely but too well,

the epigrammatic terseness of the dispatch, the dictated dispatch, begins to quiver. Then, with a rising emotional swell, description becomes unmistakably self-dramatization – self-dramatization as un-self-comprehending as before:

> Of one not easily jealous, but being wrought,
> Perplex'd in the extreme; of one whose hand,
> Like the base Indian, threw a pearl away

Richer than all his tribe; of one whose subdued eyes,
Albeit unused to the melting mood,
Drop tears as fast as the Arabian trees
Their medicinal gum.

Contemplating the spectacle of himself, Othello is overcome with the pathos of it. But this is not the part to die in: drawing himself proudly up, he speaks his last words as the stern soldier who recalls, and re-enacts, his supreme moment of deliberate courage:

Set you down this;
And say besides, that in Aleppo once,
Where a malignant and a turban'd Turk
Beat a Venetian and traduced the state,
I took by the throat the circumcised dog
And smote him, thus. (Stabs himself.)

It is a superb *coup de théâtre*.

As, with that double force, a *coup de théâtre*, it is a peculiarly right ending to the tragedy of Othello. The theme of the tragedy is concentrated in it – concentrated in the final speech and action as it could not have been had Othello 'learnt through suffering'. That he should die acting his ideal part is all in the part: the part is manifested here in its rightness and solidity, and the actor as inseparably the man of action. The final blow is as real as the blow it re-enacts, and the histrionic intent symbolically affirms the reality: Othello dies belonging to the world of action in which his true part lay.

That so many readers – Coleridge, Swinburne, Bradley, for instance – not belonging to that world should have found Othello's part irresistibly attractive, in the sense that they have preferred to see the play through Othello's eyes rather than Shakespeare's, is perhaps not after all surprising. It may be suggested that the cult of T. E. Lawrence has some relevance here. And Othello is not merely a glamorous man of action who dominates all companies, he is (as we have all been) cruelly and tragically wronged – a victim of relentless intrigue, and, while remaining noble and heroic, is allowed to appreciate the pathos of his own fate. He has, in fact, all the advantages of that last speech, where the invitation to identity oneself with him is indeed hardly resistible. Who does not (in some moments) readily see himself as the hero of such a *coup de théâtre*?

The exaltation of Iago, it has already been suggested, is a corollary of this response to Othello. What but supremely subtle villainy could have brought to this kind of ruin the hero whose perfect nobility we admire and love? Bradley concludes that

> to compare Iago with the Satan of *Paradise Lost* seems almost absurd, so immensely does Shakespeare's man exceed Milton's fiend in evil. (p. 206)

However, to be fair to Bradley, we must add that he also finds Iago decidedly less great than Napoleon.[5] Nevertheless, even if Iago hasn't 'intellectual supremacy', we are to credit him with vast 'intellectual superiority': 'in intellect . . . and in will . . . Iago *is* great' (p. 219). If we ask the believers in Iago's intellect where they find it, they can hardly point to anything immediately present in the text, though it is true that he makes some acute and cynical observations at times. The evidence of his intellect is the success of his plot: if he hadn't had an extraordinary intellect, how could he have succeeded? That is the essential argument. It is an odd kind of literary criticism. 'The skill of Iago was extraordinary,' says Bradley, 'but', he adds, with characteristic scrupulousness, 'so was his good fortune.'

Yes, so was his good fortune – until Shakespeare gave him bad. That it should be possible to argue so solemnly and pertinaciously on the assumption that Iago, his intellect and his good fortune belong, like Napoleon and his, to history, may be taken as showing that Shakespeare succeeded in making him plausible enough for the purposes of the drama. And yet even Bradley betrays certain misgivings. Noting the astonishing (when one thinks of it) contrast between the devilish reality of Iago and the impression he makes on everyone (including his wife)[6] except Roderigo, Bradley comments (p. 217):

> What further conclusions can be drawn from it? Obviously, to begin with, the inference, which is accompanied by a thrill of admiration, that Iago's powers of dissimulation and of self-control must have been prodigious....

There we have the process by which the prodigious Iago is created. But the scrupulous Bradley nevertheless records the passing doubt:

> In fact so prodigious does his self-control appear that a reader might be excused for feeling a doubt of its possibility.

Of course, it is recorded only to be overcome:

> But there are certain observations and further inferences which, apart from a confidence in Shakespeare, would remove this doubt.

Actually, if we are to be saved from these doubts (those of us who are not strengthened by this confidence in Shakespeare), we must refrain from careful observations, comparative notes and scrupulous inferences. Shakespeare's genius carries with it a large facility in imposing conviction locally, and before we ask for more than this we should make sure we know just what is being offered us in the whole. The title tells us where, in this play (it is not, of course, so in all the plays), we are to focus. As for Iago, we know from the beginning that he is a villain; the business of Roderigo tells us that. In the other scenes we have no difficulty in taking him as we are meant to take him; and we don't (at any rate in the reading, and otherwise it's the actor's problem) ask how it is that appearance and reality can have been so successfully divorced.

Considered as a comprehensibly villainous person, he represents a not uncommon kind of grudging, cynical malice (and he's given, at least in suggestion, enough in the way of grievance and motive). But in order to perform his function as dramatic machinery he has to put on such an appearance of invincibly cunning devilry as to provide Coleridge and the rest with some excuse for their awe, and to leave others wondering, in critical reflection, whether he isn't a rather clumsy mechanism. Perhaps the most serious point to be pondered is that, if Othello is to retain our sympathy sufficiently. Iago must, as devil, claim for himself an implicit weight of emotional regard that critical reflection finds him unfit to carry.

'Clumsy', however, is not the right word for anything in *Othello*. It is a marvellously sure and adroit piece of workmanship; though closely related to that judgement is the further one that, with all its brilliance and poignancy, it comes below Shakespeare's supreme – his very greatest – works.

SOURCE: *The Common Pursuit* (1952).

NOTES

1. Cf. 'We seem to be aware in it of a certain limitation, a partial suppression of that element in Shakespeare's mind which unites him with the mystical poets and with the great musicians and philosophers.' – A. C. Bradley, *Shakespearean Tragedy*, p. 185.

'*Othello* is a story of intrigue rather than a visionary statement.' – G. Wilson Knight, *The Wheel of Fire*, p. 107.

2. 'Finally, let me repeat that Othello does not kill Desdemona in jealousy, but in a convicion forced upon him by the almost superhuman art of Iago, such a conviction as any man would and must have entertained who had believed Iago's honesty as Othello did.' – Coleridge, *Essays and Lectures on Shakespeare*.

3. See that valuable book, *The Wheel of Fire*.

4. There is, I find, an admirable note on this speech in Mr T. S. Eliot's essay, 'Shakespeare and the Stoicism of Seneca'.

5. 'But compare him with one who may perhaps be roughly called a bad man of supreme intellectual power, Napoleon, and you see how mean and negative Iago's mind is, incapable of his military achievements, much more incapable of his political constructions' (p. 236).

6. 'And it is a fact too little noticed that he presented an appearance not very different to his wife. There is no sign either that Emilia's marriage was downright unhappy, or that she suspected the true nature of her husband.'

Helen Gardner

THE NOBLE MOOR (1955)

Among the tragedies of Shakespeare *Othello* is supreme in one quality: beauty. Much of its poetry, in imagery, perfection of phrase, and steadiness of rhythm, soaring yet firm, enchants the sensuous imagination. This kind of beauty *Othello* shares with *Romeo and Juliet* and *Antony and Cleopatra*; it is a corollary of the theme which it shares with them. But *Othello* is also remarkable for another kind of beauty. Except for one trivial scene with the clown, all is immediately relevant to the central issue; no scene requires critical justification. The play has a rare intellectual beauty, satisfying the desire of the imagination for order and harmony between the parts and the whole. Finally, the play has intense moral beauty. It makes an immediate appeal to the moral imagination, in its presentation in the figure of Desdemona of a love which does not alter 'when it alteration finds', but 'bears it out even to the edge of doom'. These three kinds of beauty are interdependent, since all arise from the nature of the hero. Othello's vision of the world expresses itself in what Mr Wilson Knight has called the '*Othello* music'; the 'compulsive course' of his nature dominates the action, driving it straight on to its conclusion; Othello arouses in Desdemona unshakeable love. I am unable, therefore, to accept some recent attempts to find meaning in a play, which has to more than one critic seemed to lack meaning, in its progressive revelation of the inadequacy of the hero's nobility. Such an interpretation disregards the play's most distinctive quality. It contradicts that immediate and overwhelming first impression to which it is a prime rule of literary criticism that all further analysis must conform.

A variety of critics in this century, while recognizing its poignancy, human veracity, and dramatic brilliance, have agreed in being unwilling to praise *Othello* without some reservations. Bradley found in it 'a certain limitation, a partial suppression of that element in Shakespeare's mind which unites him with the mystical poets and with the great musicians and philosophers'. Granville-Barker said of Othello that he 'goes ignorantly to his doom'. 'The mere sight of such beauty and nobility and happiness, all wickedly destroyed, must be a harrowing one. Yet the pity and terror of it come short of serving for the purgation of our souls, since Othello's own soul stays unpurged.... It is a tragedy without meaning, and that is the ultimate horror of it.' Bradley's complaint that *Othello* is unphilosophic, and Granville-Barker's, that it is 'without meaning', echo faintly the most famous of all attacks upon *Othello*. The absurd morals which Rymer found in it were a witty way of declaring it had no meaning, since Rymer equated meaning with general moral truth. The absence of general moral truth he made clear by his preposterously particular axioms. When Granville-Barker adds, 'It does not so much purge us as fill us with horror and anger.... Incongruity is the keynote of the tragedy', we are hearing a polite version of Rymer's summary judgement: 'The tragical part is plainly none other than a Bloody Farce, without salt or savour.' And Mr T. S. Eliot, whose comments on Othello's last speech[1] gave the hint for subsequent discussions of the hero as a study in self-dramatization, self-idealization, and self-deception, remarked in a note to his essay on *Hamlet* that he had never seen 'a cogent refutation of Thomas Rymer's objections to *Othello*', thus implying that he found some cogency in Rymer's attack.

There are various reasons why *Othello* should seem more remote from us than the other tragedies. A feature of Shakespearian studies in the last twenty years has been the interest in the Histories and the comparative neglect of the Comedies. The social and political ideas of the Elizabethans: the Tudor conception of history as the realm of providential judgements, the ideas of natural order, the chain of being, and 'degree, priority and place', obviously relevant to the Histories, have also some relevance to *Hamlet*, *King Lear*, and *Macbeth*. They throw some light there, though perhaps rather 'a dim religious one', and on the periphery rather than on the centre. They cast no light upon *Othello*, whose affinities are with the Comedies. We must shut up the *Book of Homilies* and *The Mirror for Magistrates* and open the love poets for a change.

Then, again, the revival of interest in allegory, and indeed of the ability to read allegory, is one of the critical achievements of this century. This has naturally influenced the interpretation of Shakespeare's plays. Whether or not allegorical and symbolical interpretations hold in other plays, they are defeated in *Othello* by the striking human individuality of the characters. What Shelley rather intemperately called 'the rigidly-defined and ever-repeated idealisms of a distorted superstition' are not to be found in a play which abounds in 'living impersonations of the truth of human passions'. It is perhaps not wholly improper to see Cordelia as Truth. But Desdemona's truth is the devotion of her whole heart to the husband of her choice, and is quite consistent humanly, but not allegorically, with her marked tendency to economize with truth. And how can one attempt to allegorize a heroine whose companion is Emilia? The attempt to treat plays as if they were poems cannot succeed with a work which so signally exemplifies Ezra Pound's distinction: 'The medium of drama is not words, but persons moving about on a stage using words.'

It has been suggested that the frequent references to Heaven and Hell, angels and devils make a theological interpretation necessary. On the contrary, their very frequency deprives them of any imaginative potency. They are a part of the play's vivid realism, setting it firmly in the contemporary world. Because Macbeth so explicitly excludes 'the life to come', we may, I think, legitimately see in his tragedy a representation of 'judgement here', analogous to what men have thought the state of the lost to be, and say that *Macbeth* makes imaginatively apprehensible the idea of damnation. In the pagan world of *King Lear*, the sudden Christian phrase 'Thou art a soul in bliss' is like the opening of a window on to another landscape. For a moment analogy is suggested, and works upon the imagination. But Heaven and Hell are bandied about too lightly in *Othello* for the words to have any but a flat ring. The only great and moving lines which look beyond the grave are Othello's

O ill-starr'd wench!
Pale as thy smock! When we shall meet at compt,
This look of thine will hurl my soul from heaven,
And fiends will snatch at it.

Damnation and salvation are outside the field of reference of a play in which the Last Day is so conceived, as the confrontation of two human beings.* When Othello exclaims

I look down towards his feet; but that's a fable.
It that thou be'st a devil, I cannot kill thee.

and Iago tauntingly replies: 'I bleed, sir; but not kill'd', the point is too explicit to be suggestive. 'Devil' is a cliché in this play, a tired metaphor for 'very bad', as 'angel' is for 'very good'. Theological conceptions help us as little as do social and political ones.

But the fundamental reason, I think, for *Othello*'s appearing of limited interest to many critics today is our distaste for the heroic, which has found little expression in our literature in this century, with the splendid exception of the poetry of Yeats. In *Othello*

* It is a little curious that members of a generation which has been so harsh to Bradley for inquiring about Lady Macbeth's children, and has rebuked Ellen Terry for speculating on how Sir Toby will get on with Maria as a wife, should pronounce so confidently on the eternal destiny of fictitious characters.

the heroic, as distinct from the exemplary and the typical: what calls out admiration and sympathy in contrast to what is to be imitated or avoided, the extraordinary in contrast to the representative, directly challenges the imagination. There are various ways in which, in discussing *Hamlet, King Lear,* and *Macbeth,* we can evade the challenge of the heroic. In *Othello* we cannot.

Othello is like a hero of the ancient world in that he is not a man like us, but a man recognized as extraordinary. He seems born to do great deeds and live in legend. He has the obvious heroic qualities of courage and strength, and no actor can attempt the role who is not physically impressive. He has the heroic capacity for passion. But the thing which most sets him apart is his solitariness. He is a stranger, a man of alien race, without ties of nature or natural duties. His value is not in what the world thinks of him, although the world rates him highly, and does not derive in any way from his station. It is inherent. He is, in a sense, a 'self-made man', the product of a certain kind of life which he has chosen to lead. In this he is in sharp contrast to the tragic hero who immediately precedes him. Hamlet is son and prince. He is in the universal situation of man born in time, creature of circumstances and duties which he has not chosen. The human relation which arises from choice is the least important in the play, or rather it is important in its failure. Hamlet the son, Ophelia the daughter, are not free to love. The possibility of freedom is the very thing which is in question in *Hamlet.* The infected will, the dubieties of moral choice, the confusions of speculation are different aspects of our sense of bondage. The gate of death is barred in *Hamlet*; man, who has not chosen to be born, cannot choose to die. The choice of death is forbidden by religion in the first soliloquy; later it is seen as a choice made impossible by our ignorance of what we choose in choosing death, so that the puzzled will cannot be absolute for life or death. At the close the hero finds death at another's hand, and not by choice.

To this vision of man bound *Othello* presents a vision of man free. The past, whose claim upon the present is at the heart of *Hamlet*, is in *Othello* a country which the hero has passed through and left behind, the scene of his 'travels' history'. The ancestors of royal siege, the father and mother, between whom the handkerchief passed and from whom it came to him, have no claim upon him. His status in Venice is contractual. The Senate are his 'very noble and approv'd good masters' because he and they have chosen it should be so. His loyalties are not the tangle of inherited loyalties, but the few and simple loyalties of choice. His duties are not the duties of his station, but the duties of his profession. Othello is free as intensely as Hamlet is unfree, and the relation which fails to establish itself in *Hamlet* is the one relation which counts here, the free relation of love. It is presented in its most extreme, that is in heroic, form, as a relation between individuals owing nothing to, and indeed triumphing over, circumstances and natural inclination. The universality of the play lies here, in its presentation of man as freely choosing and expressing choice by acts: Desdemona crossing the Senate floor to take her place beside her husband, Othello slaying her and slaying himself, Emilia crying out the truth at the cost of her life. *Othello* is particularly concerned with that deep, instinctive level where we feel ourselves to be free, with the religious aspect of our nature, in its most general sense. (This is why a theological interpretation seems so improper.) Othello's nobility lies in his capacity to worship: to feel wonder and give service.

Wonder is the note of Othello's greatest poetry, felt in the concreteness of its imagery and the firmness of its rhythms. Wonder sharpens our vision of things, so that we see them, not blurred by sentiment, or distorted by reflection, but in their own beautiful particularity. The services which he has done he speaks of at his first appearance as in the dying speech. He has taken service with the state of Venice. When it calls upon him on his marriage night he accepts, not merely without hesitation, but with alacrity: ''Tis well I am found by you.' This is the 'serious and great business' of his life, his 'occupation', source of his disciplined dignity and self-control. He is dedicated to the soldier's life of obedience and responsibility. The 'hardness' of his life gives to his sense of his own worth an impersonal dignity and grandeur. It is grounded in his sense of the worth of the life and the causes he has chosen. It is consistent with humility. This appears in the serious simplicity with which he lays before the Senate the story of his wooing, and later asks their permission, as a favour, to take his wife with him; for he is their servant and will not demand what in their need they could hardly refuse. It appears more movingly in his acknowledgement of his own 'weak merits' as a husband; and finally, most poignantly, in his image of himself as supremely fortunate, through no merit of his own stumbling upon a pearl. It is fitting that the word 'cause' should come to his lips at the crisis of his life. He has always acted for a cause. Othello is often spoken of as a man of action, in tones which imply some condescension. He is primarily a man of faith, whose faith has witnessed to itself in his deeds.

The love between Othello and Desdemona is a great venture of faith. He is free; she achieves her freedom, and at a great cost. Shakespeare, in creating the figure of her wronged father, who dies of grief at her revolt, sharpened and heightened, as everywhere, the story in the source. Her disobedience and deception of him perhaps cross her mind at Othello's ominous 'Think on thy sins.' If so, she puts the thought aside with 'They are loves I bear you.' She can no more confess herself wrong than John Donne, writing to his father-in-law: 'I knew that to have given any intimacion of it had been to impossibilitate the whole matter.' Heroic decision is seen in its rigour in the gentle Desdemona as well as in her husband.

That love as the union of free souls, freely discovering each in the other, is a mystery, inexplicable in terms of nature and society, is the assumption underlying the endless riddles, quibbles, paradoxes, and conceits of love poets, who in this age busied themselves with '*Metaphysical* Ideas and *Scholastical* Quiddities' to explain, or more frequently to make more baffling, the mystery of how 'we two being one are it'.[2] The famous double time, which has so vexed critics, though it does not trouble spectators, is in accord with this conception of love as beyond nature. That lovers' time is not the time of the seasons is a commonplace. Shakespeare laughs at it in his comedies and Donne rings endless changes on the theme. *Othello* is like an illustration to the lecture which Donne read his mistress on Love's Philosophy, comparing the growth of their love to the course of the sun, the morning shadows wearing away until 'to brave clearnesse all things are reduc'd'. But the point of the lecture was that the analogy breaks down. There is no parallel between the shadows of afternoon and evening and the shadows which fall on love:

> The morning shadowes weare away,
> But these grow longer all the day,
> But oh, loves day is short, if love decay.
>
> Love is a growing, or full constant light;
> And his first minute, after noone, is night.[3]

If love cannot perform the miracle of Joshua and make the sun stand still in the heavens, it will not suffer a slow decline. It is not in the nature of things: it has no afternoon. *Othello* is a drama of passion and runs to the time of passion; it is also a drama of love which, failing to sustain its height of noon, falls at once to night. To borrow Mr Edwin Muir's distinction, the long time belongs to the Story, the short belongs to the Fable. *Othello* is also a drama of marriage. As the hero is more than a Homeric doer of great deeds, he is more than a lover; he is a husband. Desdemona is not only the 'cunning'st pattern of excelling nature' and the girl who 'saw Othello's visage in his mind'; she is his 'true and loyal wife'. Her soul and fortunes are 'consecrated' to him. The play is not only concerned with passion and love, but with what Montaigne and other experienced observers have thought incompatibles: love and constancy.[4]

My subject being the Noble Moor, I cannot spend as long as I should wish upon his Ancient. There is an assumption current today that Iago expresses in some way a complementary view of life to Othello's. His power over Othello is said to derive from the fact that 'into what he speaks are projected the half-truths that Othello's romantic vision ignored, but of which his mind held secret knowledge'. I am quoting Miss Maud Bodkin, since she has been much quoted by later writers. She also speaks of the reader 'experiencing the romantic values represented in the hero, and recognizing, in a manner secretly, the complementary truths projected into the figure of Iago'.[5] Professor Empson has put this view more breezily:

> The thinking behind the 'melodrama' is not at all crude, at any rate if you give Iago his due. It is only because a rather unreal standard has been set up that the blow-the-gaff man can take on this extraordinary power. It is not merely out of their latent 'cynicism' that the listeners are meant to feel a certain sting of truth in Iago's claim to honesty, even in the broadest sense of being somehow truer than Othello to the facts of life.[6]

I cannot resist adapting some Johnsonian expressions and saying this is 'sad stuff'; 'the man is a liar and there's an end on't'. What Iago injects into Othello's mind, the poison with which he charges him, is either false deductions from isolated facts – she deceived her father – and from dubious generalizations – Venetian women deceive their husbands – or flat lies. Whatever from our more melancholy experiences we choose to call the facts of life, in this play there is one fact which matters, upon which the plot is built and by which all generalizations are tested:

> Moor, she was chaste; she lov'd thee, cruel Moor.

The notion that by striking a mean between the 'high-mindedness' of Othello and the 'low view' of Iago we shall arrive at a balanced view, one that is not 'crude', could only have arisen in an age which prefers to the heroic that strange idol of the abstracting intelligence, the normal, and for the 'beautiful idealisms of moral excellence' places before us the equally unattainable but far more dispiriting goal of 'adaptation to life'. But, in any case, the sum will not work out, for Iago has not a point of view at all. He is no realist. In any sense which matters he is incapable of speaking truth, because he is incapable of disinterestedness. He can express a high view or a low view to taste. The world and other people exist for him only to be used. His definition of growing up is an interesting one. Maturity to him is knowing how to 'distinguish betwixt a benefit and an injury'. His famous 'gain'd knowledge' is all generalizations, information docketed and filed. He is monstrous because, faced with the manifold richness of experience, his only reaction is calculation and the desire to manipulate. If we try to find in him a view of life, we find in the end only an intolerable levity, a power of being 'all things to all men' in a very unapostolic sense, and in incessant activity. Iago is the man of action in this play, incapable of contemplation and wholly insusceptible to the holiness of fact. He has, in one sense, plenty of motives. His immediate motives for embarking on the whole scheme are financial, the need to keep Roderigo sweet, and his desire for the lieutenancy. His general motive is detestation of superiority in itself and as recognized by others; he is past master of the sneer. Coleridge has been much criticized for speaking of his 'motiveless malignity' and yet the note of glee in Iago confirms Coleridge's moral insight. Ultimately, whatever its proximate motives, malice is motiveless; that is the secret of its power and its horror, why it can go unsuspected and why its revelation always shocks. It is, I fear, its own reward.

Iago's power is at the beginning of the action, where he appears as a free agent of mischief, creating his plot out of whatever comes to hand; after the middle of the third act he becomes the slave of the passion which he has aroused, which is the source of whatever grandeur he has in our imagination. Othello's agony turns the 'eternal villain', the 'busy and insinuating rogue', the 'cogging cozening slave' of the first acts into the 'Spartan dog, more fell than anguish, hunger, or the sea' of the close. The crisis of the action comes when Othello returns 'on the rack', determined that he will not 'make a life of jealousy', and demands that Iago furnish him with proof. Iago's life is from now on at stake. Like Desdemona's it hangs upon the handkerchief. He must go forward, to everyone's ruin and his own.

Iago ruins Othello by insinuating into his mind the question, 'How do you know?' The tragic experience with which this play is concerned is loss of faith, and Iago is the instrument to bring Othello to this crisis of his being. His task is made possible by his being an old and trusted companion, while husband and wife are virtually strangers, bound only by passion and faith; and by the fact that great joy bewilders, leaving the heart apt to doubt the reality of its joy. The strange and extraordinary, the heroic, what is beyond nature, can be made to seem the unnatural, what is against nature. This is one of Iago's tricks. But the collapse of Othello's faith before Iago's hints, refusals, retreats, reluctant avowals, though plausible and circumstantiated, is not, I believe, ultimately explicable; nor do I believe we make it so by searching for some psychological weakness in the hero which caused his faith to fail, and whose discovery will protect us from tragic experience by substituting for its pleasures the easier gratifications of moral and intellectual superiority to the sufferer. There is only one answer to Iago's insinuations, the answer Othello made to Brabantio's warning: 'My life upon her faith.' It is one thing to retort so to open enmity; more difficult to reply so to the seemingly well-meant warnings of a friend. That Othello does not or cannot reply so to Iago, and instead of making the venture of faith, challenges him to prove his wife false, is his tragic error.

Tragic suffering is suffering which a nature, by reason of its virtues, is capable of experiencing to the full, but is incapable of tolerating, and in which the excellencies of a nature are in conflict with each other. The man of conscience suffers the torment of confusion of conscience, the man of loving heart the torment of love spurned and of invasion by the passion of hatred. The one finds himself 'marshalled to knavery', the other driven to bitter curses. The man of moral imagination and human feeling will suffer the extremity of moral despair and human isolation. The man of faith is most able to experience what loss of faith is: but he is also unable to endure existence in a world where faith is dead. Othello has known 'ecstasy', which doth 'unperplex'. The loss of that leaves him 'perplexed in the extreme' and conscious of sex and sex only as 'what did move'.[7] He has seen Desdemona as his 'soul's joy'. It is intolerable to be aware in her of only what 'the sense aches at.'

Until the end is reached drama looks always ahead. If Shakespeare has, in fact, presented his hero and his love as flawed, then he has done it so subtly that I do not see how any spectator can have been aware of it. As soon as his agony is upon him we look forward to its resolution, not backwards to find some imperfection in his nature to account for his error. What matters to the tragic dramatist is wherefore, not why: not what causes suffering, but what comes of it. We distract ourselves, and to no purpose, by asking insoluble questions such as: Why 'seems it so particular' to Hamlet? Why does so small a fault in Cordelia seem so ugly to Lear? Why does a prophecy of 'things that do sound so fair' arouse in Macbeth not a glorious image of himself as a king, but a 'horrid image' of himself as a murderer?

Macbeth is not a psychological study of ambition, or, if it is, it is a singularly unilluminating one. It is about murder. *Othello* is not a study in pride, egoism, or self-deception: its subject is sexual jealousy, loss of faith in a form which involves the whole personality at the profound point where body meets spirit.

The solution which Othello cannot accept is Iago's: 'Put up with it.' This is as impossible as that Hamlet should, like Claudius, behave as if the past were done with and only the present mattered. Or that Lear should accept Goneril and Regan's view of the proper meekness of the old and, in Freud's words, should 're-nounce love, choose death, and make friends with the necessity of dying'. Or that Macbeth should attempt a tedious returning. The heroic core of tragedy is in this refusal of the hero to accommodate himself: it is why he can always be treated as a moral warning. Let Hamlet remember that 'Vengeance is the Lord's', allow the world to go its own way and mind the business of his own soul. Let Lear recognize that it is a law of life that the young should thrust out the old, and moderate his demands for love. Let Macbeth accept the human condition that life is a 'fitful fever', the future always uncertain, and there is no possibility of being 'safely thus'. Let Othello remember that perfection is not to be looked for, that though two may at times feel one, at other times they will feel very much two. Desdemona is beautiful, whether she is true or not.

But to Othello loyalty is the very principle of his moral being. He cannot say tenderly with a modern poet

> Lay your sleeping head, my love,
> Human on my faithless arm;

and accepting that

> Certainty, fidelity
> On the stroke of midnight pass
> Like vibrations of a bell,

enjoy her as

> Mortal, guilty, but to me
> The entirely beautiful.[8]

Nor, since, far from being one who lives to himself alone, his nature goes out to seek value beyond itself, can he steel his senses against her beauty. He has not the invulnerability of the proud, and cannot armour himself with the thought of his own self-sufficient virtue, arguing that 'the Honour of a true heroique spirit dependeth not upon the carriage or behaviour of a woman', and remembering that 'the Gallantest men in the world ... were all Cuckolds' and 'made no stirre about it'.[9]

Tragic responsibility can only be savoured within a fixed field of moral reference. Mercy killings, honour slayings, and innocent adulteries are not the stuff of tragedy. But tragic responsibility is not the same as moral guilt. It shows itself in Hamlet's acceptance of the imperative to stay at his post, although this involves many deaths and his own commission of acts which outrage the very conscience which impels him; in Lear's flinging out into the storm to take upon himself the role of universal sufferer and universal judge; and in Macbeth's perseverance in 'knowing the deed'. It shows itself in Othello's destruction of an idol, his decision to regain his freedom by destroying what he must desire, but cannot honour. That baser passions are mingled with this imperative to sacrifice, that in the final moment Othello kills his wife in rage, only means that in presenting man as 'an animal that worships', Shakespeare, keeping to 'the truth of human passions' presents both terms. But, in its mixture of primitive animality and agonizing renunciation, the murder of Desdemona has upon it the stamp of the heroic. It has what Yeats saw in the Easter Rising, which neither his moral nor his political judgement approved, and one of whose leaders he had disliked and despised: a 'terrible beauty', contrasting with the 'casual comedy' of daily life.

The act is heroic because Othello acts from inner necessity. Although the thought of social dishonour plays a part in his agony, it has no place in this final scene. He kills her because he cannot 'digest the poison of her flesh';[10] and also to save her from herself, to restore meaning to her beauty. The act is also heroic in its absoluteness, disinterestedness, and finality. Othello does not look beyond it. It must be done. The tragic hero usurps the functions of the gods and attempts to remake the world. This *hubris*, which arouses awe and terror, appears in an extreme form in Othello's assumption of the role of a god who chastises where he loves, and of a priest who must present a perfect victim. He tries to confess her, so that in her last moment she may be true, and suffering the death of the body as expiation may escape the death of the soul. Her persistence in what he believes to be a lie and her tears at the news of Cassio's death turn the priest into the murderer. The heroic is rooted in reality here: the godlike is mingled with the brutal, which Aristotle saw as its true opposite, and Desdemona, love's martyr, dies like a frightened child, pleading for 'but half an hour' more of life.

'I am glad I have ended my revisal of this dreadful scene. It is not to be endured', said Johnson. And yet, this terrible act has wonderful tragic rightness. Only by it can the tragic situation be finally resolved, and in tragedy it is the peace of finality which we look for. Living, Desdemona can never prove her innocence. There is nothing she can do to 'win her lord again'. She could, of course, save herself, and in so doing save her husband from crime, dishonour, and death. She could leave this terrifying monster and ask for the protection of her own countrymen, the messengers of Venice. This sensible solution never crosses her mind. She remains with the man her 'love approves', and since

> There is a comfort in the strength of love,

for all her bewilderment and distress she falls asleep,

to wake to find her faith rewarded by death. But in death she does 'win her lord again'.

Emilia's silence while her mistress lived is fully explicable in terms of her character. She shares with her husband the generalizing trick and is well used to domestic scenes. The jealous, she knows,

> are not ever jealous for the cause,
> But jealous for they are jealous.

If it was not the handkerchief it would be something else. Why disobey her husband and risk his fury? It would not do any good. This is what men are like. But Desdemona dead sweeps away all such generalities and all caution. At this sight, Emilia though 'the world is a huge thing' finds that there is a thing she will not do for it. By her heroic disregard for death she gives the only 'proof' there can be of Desdemona's innocence: the testimony of faith. For falseness can be proved, innocence can only be believed. Faith, not evidence, begets faith.

The revival of faith in Othello which rings through his last speech overrides that sense of his own guilt which we have been told he ought to be dwelling on. His own worth he sees in the services he has rendered. It is right that he should be conscious of what has given his life value when he is about to take it, as he was conscious of her beauty when about to sacrifice that. His error he cannot explain. He sees it in an image which asserts her infinite value and his supreme good fortune, which in ignorance he did not realize, accepting and translating into his own characteristic mode of thought Emilia's characteristic 'O gull! O dolt! As ignorant as dirt!' The tears he weeps now are not 'cruel tears', but good tears, natural and healing. He communicates this by an image drawn from his life of adventure. Perhaps the Arabian trees come to his mind because in that land of marvels 'the Phoenix builds her spicy nest'. Then, as he nerves himself to end everything, there flashes across his mind an image from his past which seems to epitomize his whole life and will 'report him and his cause aright'; an act of suicidal daring, inspired by his chosen loyalty to Venice. With the same swiftness he does justice on himself, traducer and murderer of his Venetian wife. As, at their reunion, after the tempest, his joy stopped his speech, so now his grief and worship express themselves finally in an act, the same act: he dies 'upon a kiss'.

No circumstances point away from this close. No living Fortinbras or Malcolm, no dead Goneril and Regan allow us to speak of a purged realm or of the justice of the heavens. There is nothing but the 'tragic loading of this bed' and the comment of the generous Cassio: 'For he was great of heart.' Yet in this terrible end there is so solemn a sense of completeness that it might well be called the most beautiful end in Shakespearian tragedy.

Each of Shakespeare's great tragedies has its own design. The ground plan of the tragedy of *Othello* is that of a tragedy of fortune, the fall of a great man from a visible height of happiness to utter loss. This is not at all the shape the story has in the source; but this is how Shakespeare saw Cinthio's powerful but sordid story of a garrison intrigue. He spent his first two acts in presenting wonder great as content, and content that is absolute, delaying the opening of his tragic conflict until his third act. The design of the tragedy of fortune has a very different effect from the design of what may be called the tragedy of dilemma, in which, as in *Hamlet*, the hero is presented to us in circumstances not of his own making, confronted with another's crime; or from the design of the tragedy of error, where the hero's initial act releases evil forces and brings enormous suffering, or from that of the tragedy of crime and retribution. We never see Hamlet prosperous. Lear's rash and cruel act opens the action. Macbeth is no sooner before us than he is in temptation, 'rapt' in inner struggle. In plays with these designs, the conclusions have something of the nature of solutions: the end answers the beginning.

In its simplest form the tragedy of fortune cannot be rationalized. It takes man out of the realm of natural causality, the steady course which birth holds on to death, showing him as the victim of the illogical, what can neither be avoided nor foreseen. To achieve its effect it glorifies human life, displaying the capacity of the human heart for joy and leaving on the mind an ineffaceable impression of splendour, thus contradicting the only moral which can be drawn from it: *Vanitas vanitatum*. *Othello* has this in common with the tragedy of fortune that the end in no way blots out from the imagination the glory of the beginning. But the end here does not merely by its darkness throw up into relief the brightness that was. On the contrary, beginning and end chime against each other. In both the value of life and love is affirmed.

But *Othello* is also pre-eminently the tragedy of a deed. The 'deed of horror', *to deinon*, which in *Hamlet* lies behind the direct action, in *Macbeth* inaugurates it, and in *King Lear* is diffused through many acts of cruelty during the middle action, is, in *Othello*, the consummation of the action. Crime and catastrophe virtually coincide. Here again the shape of the play is quite different from the shape of the story in the source. The murder of Desdemona is not an act for which Heaven will in the end provide vengeance; it is a means of immediate revelation.

Fortune has been said to be the mistress of comedy, as opposed to Destiny, the mistress of tragedy. The vision of life which Shakespeare embodied in *Othello* cannot be analysed in terms of either destiny or fortune, and this is, I think, why more than one critic has complained that the play, although thrilling, lacks 'meaning'. The hero is a great individual, with all the qualities of a tragic hero, who expresses the strength of his nature in a terrible deed. But he finds the value of his life not within himself but without himself. He is the most obviously heroic of the tragic heroes, but he is unlike the great-hearted man of Aristotle, who is 'unable to make his life revolve round another' and is not 'given to admiration'. His nobility lies in his capacity to recognize value and give loyalty. The rhythm of pure tragedy is of a single life fulfilling itself and coming to an end in death. The rhythm of pure comedy is of relationships dissolved and reformed. The truth of tragedy is that each of us in finally alone. The truth of comedy is that man's final end is union with others, that he is 'in unitie defective'.

When, at the close of the *Symposium,* Socrates defended the wild paradox that 'the same person is able to compose both tragedy and comedy and that the foundations of the tragic and comic arts were essentially the same', his audience, who were so unfortunate as to live two thousand years before he was proved to be right, 'rather convicted than convinced went to sleep'. The foundation of Shakespeare's comedy and tragedy is the conception of man as finding his fulfilment in love, and therefore as not self-sufficient, but dependent upon others. In none of Shakespeare's great tragedies is the rhythm of fate felt in its purity, with the exception of *Macbeth,* whose hero rejects chance and chooses solitude. Over *Macbeth,* which is oracular, the future, the tense of destiny, lowers. Both 'fate' and 'fortune' are spoken of in *Othello.* In *King Lear* the word 'fate' does not occur, and its shockingly capricious end has poetic not dramatic logic. The presence of comedy 'universal, ideal and sublime' in *King Lear* made Shelley award it the palm over the masterpieces of the ancient world, the *Agamemnon* and the *Oedipus Rex.* For Shelley, though he does not make the connexion, believed that the 'great secret of morals is love'.

In *Othello* the two rhythms are so finely poised against each other that if we listen to either without the other we impoverish the whole. Othello is the tragic hero, fulfilling his destiny, who comes to the limit, 'the very sea-mark of his utmost sail', expressing his whole nature in a tragic act. He is the comic hero, discovering at the close a truth he knew at the beginning, and so he appears, dazed and blundering beneath the scourge of Emilia's tongue, remote for the time from our sympathy. Should the course of his life be described as a pilgrimage to a goal, or is it a straying from a centre which he finds again in death? Such straying is of the essence of life, whose law is change. Failures and recoveries of faith are the rhythm of the heart, whose movement is here objectified and magnified for our contemplation. If the old saying is true 'Qui non zelat non amat', then the greater love is, the greater jealousy will be. Perfect love casts out fear; but beneath the moon, mistress of change, only in death can

> Beauty, truth, and rarity,
> Grace in all simplicity,

be safe from mistaking, and constancy find its true image. The close of *Othello* should leave us at peace, for

> Death is now the phoenix' nest;
> And the turtle's loyal breast
> To eternity doth rest.

The significance of *Othello* is not to be found in the hero's nobility alone, in his capacity to know ecstasy, in his vision of the world, and in the terrible act to which he is driven by his anguish at the loss of that vision. It lies also in the fact that the vision was true. I cannot agree to find lacking in meaning this most beautiful play which sems to have arisen out of the same mood as made Keats declare: 'I am certain of nothing but of the holiness of the Heart's affections and the truth of Imagination.'

SOURCE: *Proceedings of the British Academy,* XLI.

NOTES

1. See 'Shakespeare and the Stoicism of Seneca', a lecture delivered in 1927, reprinted in *Selected Essays* (1932). Mr Eliot was making a general comment on

Elizabethan tragic heroes and took this speech as an extreme example. His comment touches, I think, all tragic heroes, and not merely Elizabethan ones. It raises the whole question of how the characters in a poetic drama present themselves, of the self-consciousness of the tragic hero by which he creates himself in our imagination.

2. Donne, 'The Canonization':

> The Phoenix riddle hath more wit
> By us, we two being one, are it.
> So, to one neutrall thing both sexes fit.

3. Donne, 'A Lecture upon the Shadow'.

4. 'It is against the nature of love, not to be violent, and against the condition of violence to be constant' (*Essays*, iii 5). Cf. Iago's 'It was a violent commencement in her, and thou shalt see an answerable sequestration.'

5. *Archetypal Patterns in Poetry* (1934) pp. 223 and 333. When Miss Bodkin writes that as psychological critics we must note that the plot is built 'not merely on falsehoods . . . but also on partial truths of human nature that the romantic vision ignores' and cites as examples of such 'truths' that 'a woman, "a super-subtle Venetian", suddenly wedding one in whom she sees the image of her ideal warrior, is liable to experience moments of revulsion' and that 'a woman's love may be won, but not held, by "bragging and telling her fantastical lies"', the irrelevance of psychological criticism, which generalizes and abstracts, where drama particularizes, is obvious. Whatever truth there may be in these two generalizations the plot is built on their untruth in this case.

6. *The Structure of Complex Words* (1951) p. 248.

7. Donne, 'The Extasie':

> This Extasie doth unperplex
> (We said) and tell us what we love,
> We see by this, it was not sexe,
> We see, we saw not what did move.

8. W. H. Auden, *Look Stranger* (1936) p. 43.

9. 'The more discretion a man hath, the lesse shall hee bee troubled with these franticke fits; and seeing, as a certaine noble Gentleman sayth, the Honour of a true heroique spirit dependeth not upon the carriage or behaviour of a woman, I see no reason why the better sort should take this false playing of their Wives so much at the heart as they doe, especially, when it is their Destinie, and not Desert, to be so used. *Montaigne,* that brave French Barron, being of this minde; for saith he, the Gallantest men in the world, as *Lucullus, Caesar, Anthony, Cato,* and such like Worthies, were all Cuckolds; yea, and (which was more) knew it, although they made no stirre about it: neither was there in all that time, but one Gull, and Coxcombe, and that was *Lepidus,* that dyed with the anguish thereof.' Marginal note by Robert Toft in his translation of Benedetto Varchi: *The Blazon of Jealousie* (1615) p. 29. The reference is to Montaigne, *Essays,* iii 5.

10. Cf. Adriana in *The Comedy of Errors,* II ii 144–8:

> I am possess'd with an adulterate blot;
> My blood is mingled with the crime of lust:
> For if we two be one and thou play false,
> I do digest the poison of thy flesh,
> Being strumpeted by thy contagion.

John Bayley

LOVE AND IDENTITY: *OTHELLO* (1962)

. . . The initial fallacy of much *Othello* criticism is the assumption that it is a simple clear-cut affair, and that the task of the critic is to determine what kind of simplicity, so to speak, is involved. For Wilson Knight it is the simplicity of intrigue; for Leavis, that of a special kind of character study; for Bradley (whose approach is less narrowly perspicacious and therefore less inadequate), the more exciting simplicity of a fathomless evil corrupting, though not eclipsing, good. The strong feelings aroused are all directed to one of these particular ends. But if we rather assume, from the nature of the subject and of the response we give to it, that the play is likely to be a highly complex affair, with a Shakespearean variety of perceptions and significances, then we shall cease to be merely pro- or anti-Othello, or under the spell of a *coup de théâtre,* and instead be more receptive to its totality of effect. It is this effect that we must now look at in greater detail.

In claiming for the play a far greater degree of complexity than is generally assumed, I am not saying that it closely resembles Shakespeare's other great plays, or that it works in the same way as they do. *Othello* is a tragedy of incomprehension, not at the level of intrigue but at the very deepest level of human dealings. And one would expect that the effect of such a tragedy would be significantly different from those in which a kind of understanding links the actors ever more closely as they suffer or inflict suffering; that it would be, in fact, more like that of a great novel. No one in *Othello* comes to understand himself or anyone else. None of them realize their situation. At the centre, between the poles of the play, Desdemona, Cassio, and Emilia show common sense and humanity, but it is more a matter of good instinct than illumination. Iago maintains to the end the dreadful integrity of his own ignorance, and in spite of – or perhaps because of – the revelation of Desdemona's innocence, Othello retains to the end his agonized incomprehension – the incomprehension which is so moving an aspect of tragedy in sexual love. His love for Desdemona was to him a marvellous revelation of himself rather than a real knowledge of her. And the proof of her innocence is no substitute for such an awareness. This is the final tragic separation, intensified by the conviction that she is going to heaven and he is going to hell. But although the characters never achieve understanding, and although our response to them – as theirs to each other – shifts with the successive and conflicting pulls of emotion and analysis, so that we see Othello through his own eyes and Iago's as well as with our own, yet if we wait for the fullness of what the play has to offer we do reach a state of tragic comprehension; we are left with a greater insight into the passions and the will, and how they operate to cut us off from each other and from ourselves.

The way this happens is however, as I have suggested, unique in Shakespeare. The tragic atmosphere offers none of that harmonious and formal communion in sorrow which plays at the end of *King Lear*,[1] or the participation in *Macbeth* at the re-establishment of spiritual order. Othello's tragedy is personal, ending in a total lonelines of spirit, and our recognition of it can only be correspondingly solitary. A parallel with the essentially private revelation of the novel form is always making itself felt. The critical approaches we have been considering imply that the other tragedies are more characteristically and greatly Shakespearean because they are more susceptible to the kind of exegesis which the criticism prefers. Because of his enthusiasm for what he regards as its symbolic presentation of Renaissance Man, Wilson Knight leaves us with the impression that *Timon of Athens* is the most remarkable of Shakespeare's tragedies. His interpretative method finds so much to elicit that the sense of proportion overreaches itself. It is this feeling for the material available to criticism which has produced the concept – now almost a cliché in Shakespearean criticism – of 'different imaginative levels' within the working of the greatest kind of tragedy. Thus Hamlet, for instance, is at the surface a gripping masterpiece of suspense and murder; rather deeper down it reveals the psychological relationship of father, mother, and son; deeper still, perhaps, the quasi-religious dilemma of a man who suddenly finds himself at odds with the seeming reality of the world. Except at the surface the exact nature of these 'levels' will of course be perpetually disputed and seen in different lights, but the idea of them does suggest the inexhaustibility of our experience of Shakespeare. Their chief drawback, like the critique of 'impersonality', is the tendency to be invoked as a tragic standard which Othello, simple and undifferentiated as befits a story of intrigue, is again found to fall short of.

Modern criticism here is ignoring the unfamiliar effect because it does not see the familiar one it is looking for. The 'levels' of Othello are temporal (to use Wilson Knight's terminology), not spatial; and they are not those of mutually inclusive 'meanings' but of successive and at first mutually exclusive points of view. Hamlet is at one and the same moment a revenge hero, an Oedipal hero, and a religious hero: the rôles can all be played together and all are in some sense true; and though an audience could hardly in practice take them all in simultaneously, the possibility of this is a valid aim and convention. Moreover, while for Leavis, as for Bradley, Othello is either a jealous brute or he is not, the most opinionated critic would concede that most attitudes towards Hamlet and most qualities imputed to him are reconcilable in the total tragic effect. But the whole tendency of *Othello* is to make us partisan, to underline the incommensurability of opposed emotional stances. Just as Desdemona can never see Othello as Iago does, or Iago as does Desdemona, so our own succession of responses follows and reflects the partial and solipsistic attitudes of the protagonists. We are in the bafflingly relative world of social observation, where our own passions and prejudices distort reality as much as those of the people we are watching; and where our discernment of an unconscious motive or a comical lack of awareness – 'A's good nature is really selfishness', or, 'Does B ever realize how he bores?' – also reveals our own nature and desires to others who may themselves be noting our unawareness of the fact. In *Othello* love is the agent which precipitates and co-ordinates these responses, keeps them moving, and forces us to reflect in the privacy of our own feelings the stages of an isolated and mysterious struggle.

For love is of all forces in society the most confusing and the most revealing; it stands both for the frightful difficulty of knowing other people and for the possibility of that knowledge; its existence implies the ideal existence of understanding and its absence the total removal of it. The stages of our response to *Othello* compel us to see both with the eye of love and without it, and it is our awareness of what this means that leads us at last to a settled appraisal. The fatal thing is to get stuck at some point, to come to a halt on some premature conviction about the nature of the play, an easy course for the critic whose instinct it is to make up his mind about the nature of the experience he is having. Like all great works of art, *Othello* deprives us of the confident sense of ourselves *vis-à-vis* the rest of the world.

'Mutually exclusive points of view' is a phrase which might seem to imply an almost Shavian dramatic mode – lively argument about the nature of sexual love. But an audience gives an 'interested' and 'stimulated' response to *Candida*, while – as the critics have shown us – Othello arouses passionate and complex emotions. The 'points of view' in *Othello* have the whole man behind them and not just an argument; an obvious distinction, but worth making in view of the contrasts in the play between poetry and prose – the most important of our pairs of 'opposing poles' already mentioned. Poetry has a great deal more to do here than in the more organically conceived tragedies, the more so because it is not so native to the world of Othello as to the court of Lear and the castle of Macbeth. *Othello* begins at the moment when the fairy-story ends, and the great 'love-duet' at the beginning of Act II announces what should be the post-marriage *détente*: it is the prelude to domesticity, 'suckling fools and chronicling small beer'. The verse must celebrate in heroic terms a domestic situation too realistic even for comedy. But it does not only celebrate it and lift it to a heroic plane, it also analyses it. Although poetry and prose are so sharply differentiated both have the power to dissect and reveal. The antithesis is not, as might be supposed, between simple colourful heroic poetry, and mordant prose, but between the natures of the prose speaker and the poetry speaker. The poetry can be complex and pointed, but it also exalts – as the prose cannot – the bountiful glory and excitement of love. That this excitement has its dangers, even its ugliness and absurdity, both poetry and prose can convey in their separate ways. In using the term 'love-duet' I am suggesting that the unique indicative function of the poetry is indeed comparable with the *aria*: Verdi's *Otello* is the most successful of all operas based on poetic drama, and the greatest performance of Othello was given by Salvini, an actor whose voice and bearing were trained in opera. The magnificence of the poetry embodies the vital splendours of love – Desdemona's at well as Othello's – and is used by those who, like Cassio and the Gentlemen at the beginning of Act II, admire and extol such love. It is not used, except as a conscious and horrible parody, by Iago, who as we have seen produces his own style of verse in deliberate opposition to the love-idiom, a style uncannily prescient of the 18th century. Emilia has her own idiom, essentially prose though formally in blank verse, for her important and trenchant speech (Act IV, scene iii) on the need for give and take between men and women.

Act II, scene i illustrates these points in detail. First Montano and the Gentlemen celebrate in the language of love the storm at sea, that 'storm of fortunes' which the lovers expected and surmounted with such triumphant confidence.

For do but stand upon the foaming shore,
The chiding billow seems to pelt the clouds;
The wind-shaked surge, with high and monstrous mane,
Seems to cast water on the burning bear,
And quench the guards of the ever-fixed pole:
I never did like molestation view
On the enchaféd flood.

In Cinthio's story the couple arrive 'on a perfectly tranquil sea', a detail only too much in keeping with the humdrum setting and the harmony of their previous conjugal life. Shakespeare's contrasting storm brings in the powers of love and danger – the latter in both its new and old senses. Cassio now arrives and thanks the previous speakers.

Thanks, you the valiant of this warlike isle,
That so approve the Moor! O, let the heavens
Give him defence against the elements,
For I have lost him on a dangerous sea.

Valiancy and love are connected, their language the same: and with the entry of Cassio the chorus swells to include Desdemona in a paean of praise.

. . . he hath achieved a maid
That paragons description and wild fame;
One that excels the quirks of blazoning pens,
And in the essential vesture of creation
Does tire the ingener.

The storm is emphasized once more:

Tempests themselves, high seas and howling winds,
The gutter'd rocks and congregated sands –
Traitors ensteept to enclog the guiltless keel –
As having sense of beauty, do omit
Their mortal natures, letting go safely by
The divine Desdemona.

And the power of love is invoked for all its votaries:

Great Jove, Othello guard,
And swell his sail with thine own powerful breath,
That he may bless this bay with his tall ship,
Make love's quick pants in Desdemona's arms,
Give renew'd fire to our extincted spirits
And bring all Cyprus comfort!

The paean reaches its climax with the appearance of Desdemona herself,

O, behold,
The riches of this ship is come on shore!
Ye men of Cyprus, let her have your knees.
Hail to thee, lady, and the grace of heaven
Before, behind thee, and on every hand,
Enwheel thee round!

It is then abruptly checked and reversed by the presence of Iago. The whole atmosphere of the scene changes at once. Cassio, the noble and enthusiastic leader of the chorus, now appears almost absurd as he administers a gallant peck to the cheek of Emilia, observing

'tis my breeding
That gives me this bold show of courtesy.

The little fatuity is endearing enough in its way, but with Iago there Cassio appears in a different light: we see him to some extent through Iago's eyes. We also realize that Cassio has an idea of himself as a well-bred person which can appear fitting and noble or as something a bit vulgar and even – in a comical way – calculating. Conscious as we are of ideas about personal identity, the *persona* and so forth, we should recognize the swiftness and accuracy with which Shakespeare makes his point about them here and connects it, *via* the realistic and operatic contrasts of the scene, with the enthusiasm and the poetry of love. Love, we might say, brings to a head this problem of identity, and also makes it seem to those in the grip of love a problem to which the answer must instantly be found. Our awareness of Cassio in this scene foreshadows the sense of him that Othello will soon come to have, and furthermore our mixed impression of Cassio as the celebrant of love foreshadows our impressions of Othello himself.

For the next hundred lines or so Iago dominates the gathering. The theme of the passage is 'placing' people in terms of parlour witticisms.

> DESDEMONA: *What wouldst thou write of me if thou shouldst praise me?*
> IAGO: *O gentle lady do not put me to't,*
> *For I am nothing if not critical.*

Desdemona enters the game in order to conceal her anxiety for Othello.

> DESDEMONA: *Come on, assay. – There's one gone to the harbour?*
> IAGO: *Ay Madam.*
> DESDEMONA: *I am not merry, but I do beguile*
> *The thing I am by seeming otherwise.*
> *– Come, how wouldst thou praise me?*

In concealing her fears from the two men Desdemona shows her instinctive consideration. She will not embarrass them by making them feel they should try to reassure her, and what she feels for Othello is no affair of theirs. The coarse common sense and home-speaking of Iago is at the furthest possible remove from her love and anxiety: it is soothing at a crisis as neutral and indifferent things are. It is conveniently to hand and she embraces it with something like zest. Again the realism of the touch makes just the right point. Unlike Cassio, whose case is more ambiguous, Desdemona 'by seeming otherwise' only reveals more clearly and poignantly to the audience 'the thing she is'. But her behaviour *could* be seen in another light: through Iago's eyes we see her responses merely reflecting his own *idées fixes* about women, and behind Iago the anguish of Othello again begins to take shape.

At the end of the Iago passage Cassio again becomes the noble chorus introducing the entrance of Othello. *Lo, where he comes!* The phrase is often met in the tragedies and establishes an entrance with wonderful economy: our obligatory use of the continuous present has deprived us of such naturally ceremonial effects. Iago will use the same phrase when he sees Othello upon the rack.

Look, where he comes! Not poppy nor mandragora
Nor all the drowsy syrups of the world
Shall ever medicine thee to that sweet sleep
Which thou owedst yesterday.

Iago is deliberately parodying the ceremonial love-idiom of Othello, Cassio, and the others, and the lines reminiscent of Othello's own sonorous style are spoken with mocking glee. The note of parody is emphasized further on in the scene, where Iago produces a horrible simulacrum of Othello's oath of vengeance:

OTHELLO: *...Like to the Pontic sea*
Whose icy currents and compulsive course
Ne'er feels retiring ebb, but keeps due on
To the Propontic and the Hellespont;
Even so my bloody thoughts, with violent pace,

Shall ne'er look back, ne'er ebb to humble love
Till that a capable and wide revenge
Swallow them up. Now, by yond marble heaven,
In the due reverence of a sacred vow
I here engage my words.

IAGO: *Do not rise yet.*
Witness, you ever-burning lights above,
You elements that clip us round about,
Witness that here Iago doth give up
The execution of his wit, hands, heart,
To wronged Othello's service. Let him command,
And to obey shall be in the remorse,
What bloody business ever.

The difference between the monumental fervour of Othello's love–hate, and Iago's melodramatic imitation of it, would hardly need commenting on if Eliot and Leavis had not suggested that this liability to parody is the weakness of Othello's poetic idiom, a weakness that reveals the hollowness of the man. Leavis takes Bradley to task for saying that Othello is 'the greatest poet' of all Shakespeare's heroes, and observes very justly that not only do other people in the play speak in the characteristic Othello style, but that 'if characters in poetic drama speak poetry we ought to be able to notice the fact without concluding that they are poets'. Certainly we ought, but where *Othello* is concerned we might also reflect that if certain characters speak poetry it is because it is the idiom of the love theme in the play. This is so obvious that the evasion of it by Eliot and Leavis seems inexplicable, until we remember their essentially negative approach to the play's presentation of love. The poetry of *Othello* is firmly and positively poetic, and so convinced is Leavis of the negative psychological purpose of the play that he is compelled to distinguish between Othello's poetical utterance when it shows 'an attitude *towards* the emotion expressed – an attitude of a kind we are familiar with in the analysis of sentimentality', and the poetry – spoken either by him or by others – which is impersonally 'in the heroic mode', and therefore genuine, its 'firm outline' not concealing an underlying softness. This distinction has no real existence. The 'heroic mode' *is* the love mode, as Dr Leavis must surely have seen if he were not so determined that love in the play is a negative and hollow thing, existing only to be shown up. The power of which the poetry is the expression and symbol is all of a piece, and conveys love in all its aspects – terrible, tender, romantic, domestic, etc. Leavis's contention that 'the heroic mode' – as distinct from the hollow and self-revealing rhetoric of Othello – has only a comparatively simple magnificence, is not borne out by a speech like Desdemona's before the senate.

That I did love the Moor to live with him
My downright violence and storm of fortunes
May trumpet to the world: my heart's subdued
Even to the very quality of my lord:
I saw Othello's visage in his mind
And to his honours and his valiant parts
Did I my soul and fortunes consecrate....

The tone is certainly joyous and magnificent, but it is also as 'revealing' as Leavis claims Othello's rhetoric to be. It reveals Desdemona's mode of being in love, just as Othello's speeches reveal his. As well as being lyrical and romantic, the love-idiom is an expository medium so sensitive that the characters who use it cannot open their mouths without revealing their emotional bias, and their conscious or unconscious conceptions of love. The criticism that emphasizes its romantic simplicity – (Wilson Knight's phrase, 'the *Othello* music', suggests the Paterian idea of poetry aspiring towards the musical condition) – fails to see its dramatic point.

The reason for this failure lies in Iago's parodying,

for I. A. Richards made what has proved to be an influential critical pronouncement when he declared that poems which can be parodied by a 'confrontation with their opposite' are necessarily on a lower poetic level than poems which have, so to speak, a built-in irony that anticipates other responses and contains many shades of feeling. Thus Landor's *Rose Aylmer* is intrinsically inferior to Scott's *Proud Maisie*, because its author sticks his neck out in a simple attitude that invites mimicry. But whatever we may feel about this criterion, it clearly cannot have any relevance to Shakespeare's dramatic poetry, whose simplicity (if it is simple) is not that of the author. Moreover we must remind ourselves again of the peculiar operation of the play, its mode of involving us in successive emotions and attitudes comparable to those of the characters themselves, and its sequential rather than simultaneous mode of illumination – a mode entailed on Shakespeare, as we have seen, by the intrigue at its roots. The magnificence of the love-choruses may indeed hypnotize us at the outset, and postpone our reception of the vital information they contain, but we shall understand them later as part of the full complexity of the *Othello* world, the world of human love and lovelessness, of the inability of one kind of love to understand another, and of the persistence with which human beings cling to the conception of their love as a part of themselves.

As her speech before the senate shows, Desdemona's way of being in love is as clearly revealed as that of Othello. The love-duet in Act II, scene i adds further touches of significance.

OTHELLO: *O my fair warrior!*
DESDEMONA: *My dear Othello!*
OTHELLO: *It gives me wonder great as my content*
To see you here before me. O my soul's joy,
If after every tempest come such calms
May the winds blow till they have wakened death!

And let the labouring bark climb hills of seas
Olympus-high, and duck again as low
As hell's from heaven! If it were now to die
'Twere now to be most happy, for I fear
My soul hath her content so absolute
That not another comfort like to this
Succeeds in unknown fate.

DESDEMONA: *The heavens forbid*
But that our loves and comforts should increase
Even as our days do grow!

OTHELLO: *Amen to that, sweet powers!*
I cannot speak enough of this content,
It stops me here, it is too much of joy:
And this, and this, the greatest discords be (kissing her)
That e'er our hearts shall make!

Two different kinds of love are movingly displayed here. Othello's is the masculine and romantic: his opening hyperbole invokes the romantic commonplace – 'Love calls to war' – and also receives Desdemona into his wholly martial personality, just as she had wished in refusing to remain 'a moth of peace'. The glory of the achievement is carried buoyantly on in the image of the ship riding the waves. What battles and dangers wouldn't they undergo for this? But then with the imagined calm a note of brooding appears; the tone changes and deepens; 'If it were now to die. . . .' Othello has withdrawn his delighted gaze from Desdemona and is addressing himself and his own vision of love. And in the romantic context that vision has an alarming familiarity. Having achieved his desire, Othello turns naturally to the idea of the *Liebestod,* death as the only fit and comparable peer of love. How can the tension otherwise be kept up and the lover remain at the summit of his happiness? Unknowingly Othello is applying this fatal romantic logic, which will not compromise possession with the trivialities of domesticity. And it is of course as a possession, a marvellous and unexpected conquest, that he sees Desdemona. He has won her like a fortune or a battle.

If heaven had made me such another jewel,
One whole entire and perfect chrysolite,
I'd not have changed her for it.

This attitude earns him the disapproval of Eliot and Leavis; but so far from singling out Othello as a type of the ignorant and ungentle lover, Shakespeare portrays him as epitomizing the positive glory of love, which like the glory of war includes and assumes the fact of suffering and injustice. Both love and war are summed up in the image of storm, a manifestation both glorious and terrifying. Yet, as we are finding, there is more in the love-duet than the poetic symbol of the storm and the poetic prolepsis of the lovers' death: there is also the sharp illumination of what men and women in love are like. Othello's sentiments are magnificently commonplace; for he shares with most men the delight of achievement and possession and he feels too the loss of freedom, of the 'unhoused condition', a loss which he has already faced in his large way and put aside. The romantic dangers are there, as with most men, but they do not diagnose his amatory weakness or label him finally. He is not a Tristan or a Lancelot, wholly committed to an intensity in love which is unaware of any freedom outside itself.

Indeed the possibility of development, and the sense of freedom that goes with it, is precisely what the duet most poignantly holds out. Desdemona's love for Othello is also of course wildly romantic – he personifies for her all the romance she has discovered to exist in life – but committing herself to this vision is for her a more matter-of-fact business than it could be for him. Her greeting is as whole-hearted as his, and as characteristic. 'My dear Othello!' – the simple warmth reveals a whole world of feminine actuality behind the male need for hyperbole and symbol. She takes his speech lightly, as the sort of wonderfully gratifying and romantic thing he *would* say – its deeper note doesn't mean much to her except as a stimulus to 'touch wood' and to give her own settled and happy conception of the future. She takes up the word 'comfort' from his speech, the sort of word which in her vision of things presents a concrete and lasting reassurance and satisfaction. The situation has a joyful sense of mutual possibility, the spaciousness which throughout the play is the atmosphere and element of love. Othello's unconsciously romantic sense of an end rather than a beginning is not final: Desdemona's placid confidence touches and lights his own, and he shows the beginnings of a readiness to draw certainty and stability from her, just as she had drawn fire and enthusiasm from him. But this interdependence is not the same as understanding: the singers in the duet are too preoccupied with the vision of their own love really to perceive the nature of their partner's. Desdemona is as much imprisoned in her assumption of love as is Othello in his, and for the same reasons: their kinds of love have produced the relationship in which they find themselves. The helplessness of Desdemona as the tragic climate darkens round her is as much emphasized as is that of Othello in the grip of his jealousy, and it proceeds from the same cause. She cannot break out of her kind of love to tell him what a monster he is being any more than he can break out of his to reflect that after all she is a free agent, and that perhaps a quiet talk would clear the matter up.

I may seem here to be seeing Shakespeare through the spectacles of Proust, for whom A can never love B but only his idea of B, and *vice versa,* with confusing and depressing results. But though one would expect the two writers to corroborate each other's vision at some points, Proust's dogmatic authority, reposing as it does on methods of analysis copied from science and philosophy, is foreign to Shakespeare, and its illuminations are of a quite different order to those of *Othello.* In the enclosed world of Proust the idea of freedom depends on the universality of error: people and their emotions seem endless because of the infinite number of ways one can get them wrong. As a hypothesis about love 'Proust's Law' is abstract and rigid: it admits no outlet, while Shakespeare's poetry not only indicates with extraordinary compression and subtlety comparable facts about love but also celebrates its infinite potentiality, a freedom based not on error but on the absence of definition. Confined in their separate visions, the lovers do not 'place' each other; their incomprehension is, paradoxically, a form of spaciousness, and it is this which Shakespeare manifests as a positive glory. Nothing is fixed and fated, because of the largeness of love's world, the sheer quality of room it makes available. The magnificence of Othello and his impression of physical size, the sweep of seas and continents that are built up behind him, the heroic Odysseys and adventures of his past – all are there to emphasize the unbounded possibilities of love, and they are brought to an almost Hegelian confrontation with an equally undeniable aspect of love – its confinement in the prison of separate egos.

The fact that both Othello and Desdemona cling at all costs to their own apprehension of love gives its shape and meaning to the last act of the tragedy. Their deaths are the very opposite of the romantic *Liebestod*, but the irony of this is infinitely deeper and truer to human experience, and for that reason strikes us with the greater compassion. Death confirms their separation in love, not their union. In his jealousy Othello accepted Iago's version of Desdemona.

I know our country disposition well.
In Venice they do let heaven see the pranks
They dare not show their husbands.

He has permitted the spaciousness of his own love vision to be enclosed in this horrible 'placing' of the loved object. For Othello has not placed Desdemona objectively at all, and into the vacuum is dropped the deadly little miniature of Iago. With a few touches Iago fills in the portrait of a Venetian deb: the promiscuity taken for granted in her set, the sexual gratification of being possessed by a real he-man, the craze for novelty which real inconvenience would soon scare back into the orthodoxy of class. It has been well said that if the villainy of Iago is impenetrable by convention, Shakespeare also makes it so in fact. His picture of Desdemona has all the more unspeakable plausibility because he really believes all women are like that. He is inventing something that comes naturally to him. And his portrait of Desdemona demoralizes Othello completely well before he begins to manufacture the actual proofs of betrayal. For Othello has apprehended Desdemona as a marvellous mirror through which to see his own experience.

> *She loved me for the dangers I had passed;*
> *And I loved her that she did pity them.*

Desdemona gives a meaning to all that has happened to him; the sudden revelation of the importance and splendour of his past is a dazzling thing, which he had taken for granted and never seen in this way before. This revelation is in a sense a loss of innocence: it brings self-consciousness and confers upon him the dramatic part which he can most naturally play. But it is also one of the great positive gifts of love. Desdemona has given it to him and he loves her for it, but ironically the very magnificence of the gift obscures the giver, for the gift – Othello himself – seems to both of them so much more actual than she. Desdemona's sense of Othello is so much more real to both of them than is the sense of Desdemona to either.

Without overdoing the *argumentum ad hominem* we can all recognize the generalized force of this, and we recognize the process involved in observations like 'he's been a different man since he met her'. Even Iago allows the phenomenon to exist as a kind of absurdity, grounds for the usual snigger. Just after the love-duet he says to Roderigo, 'If thou be'st valiant – as they say base men being in love have then a nobility in their natures more than is native to them – list me.' *Valiant* is the epithet so liberally applied to Othello in the early love-choruses, and Roderigo has his function as a kind of feeble echo, debased but still recognizable, of Othello – an echo and not a parody, for there is no mockery involved: he is a poor relation in love, not absolutely stripped of dignity even when his passion – like Othello's – makes him Iago's dupe. Love gives a natural rightness to some of his assumptions, as he shows when Iago asks him with a leer if he noticed Cassio take Desdemona's hand. 'Yes, that I did; but that was but courtesy.' He and Cassio, and Othello too, talk the same language, which is outside Iago's comprehension.

One reason for the relevance of the novel-like query: Would the lovers have settled down to a happy marriage? – is Othello's response to Desdemona's support of Cassio, an episode significantly distinct from Iago's initial suggestions, although Iago's betrayal of Cassio was of course the cause of it. We hear of it first from Emilia as she chats to Cassio.

> *– all will sure be well;*
> *The general and his wife are talking of it*
> *And she speaks for you stoutly: the Moor replies*
> *That he you hurt is of great fame in Cyprus*
> *And great affinity, and that in wholesome wisdom*
> *He might not but refuse you, but he protests he loves you*
> *And needs no other suitor but his likings*
> *To take the safest occasion by the front*
> *To bring you in again.*

At second hand thus the scene comes none the less clearly before us. In her brisk artless way, which reveals a complete lack of knowledge of Othello and his mode of love, Desdemona takes his old friend's part and brings the business up at a moment when the lovers might suitably be concerned with nothing but each other. The chill of this, somewhat drolly conveyed as it is through the medium of Emilia, might be felt by any lover as well as Othello; and the hint that he did his best to push it outside the scope of their mutuality would seem an equally human reaction. The next scene contrasts with the love-duet in its slight but painful suggestion of a discord: their mutuality is no longer perfectly synchronized, for the excellent and commonplace reason that an outside element – neutral and not in itself inimical – prevents the exact intermeshing of the gears.

DESDEMONA: *How now, My Lord!*
I have been talking with a suitor here,
A man that languishes in your displeasure.
OTHELLO: *Who is't you mean?*
DESDEMONA: *Why, your lieutenant, Cassio.*

Desdemona makes a rhetorical show of mystification, one of those nearly meaningless little demonstrations which none the less convey that the speaker knows she is not being quite straightforward. Perhaps aware of its slight tiresomeness, Othello deliberately ignores her gambit. His query is brusque. It provokes her to a greater formality and a more defensive eloquence. The whole thing, economical as it is, catches exactly the note of connubial exchanges.

Why, this is not a boon!
'Tis as I should entreat you wear your gloves,
Or feed on nourishing dishes, or keep you warm,
Or sue to you to do a peculiar profit
To your own person.

Love is no longer talking in the symbolic idiom through which Othello apprehends it. With its touchingly matter-of-fact solicitude, the speech conveys no impression of the Desdemona with whom Othello discovered his own past and personality. On the contrary it is an intrusion comparable to that of the Cassio topic, and it brings Othello's latent irritation to a head.

> *I will deny thee nothing:*
> *Whereon, I do beseech thee, grant me this,*
> *To leave me but a little to myself.*

Committed as she is, it is natural and agreeable to her to yield the point,

> *Shall I deny you? no, farewell, my lord ...*
> *Emilia, come. Be as your fancies teach you;*
> *Whate'er you be, I am obedient.*

Her sweetness produces a warmer reply from him, and the parting is on a friendlier, more understanding note. They are already beginning to learn give and take in such matters. It is the more important to realize this because of a common misunderstanding arising from Othello's next words.

> *Excellent wretch! Perdition catch my soul,*
> *But I do love thee, and when I love thee not*
> *Chaos is come again.*

Some early critics, and many later ones too, have assumed this to mean that 'the poison of jealousy has already begun to work in Othello'. But in Elizabethan English *wretch* was a word of total and unambiguous endearment. Collier aptly remarks 'such words are resorted to when those implying love, admiration, and delight, seem inadequate', and Dr Johnson is equally emphatic. There is the further point that 'when', like the German *wenn*, has here the sense of 'if'. What is significant about the speech is not a display of jealousy by Othello, but his sudden awareness of the nature of his feelings and the insubstantiality of love. What is his love exactly, and where is it to be found? Desdemona's sweetness and domestic solicitude in the glove speech cannot at this moment reassure him, because they are not what he means by love: they so emphatically do not present him with the settled and splendid figure whose reflection he once caught in her eye. He no longer sees his visage in her mind. It disturbs the unthinking and unshakeable confidence which he once had in himself, and which he effortlessly retained at the stormy climax of his fortunes. The armed meeting with Brabantio epitomized this confidence.

> *Keep up your bright swords, for the dew will rust them.*
> *Good signior, you shall more command with years*
> *Than with your weapons.*

But now the vision and the harmony are in abeyance and are replaced by the uncertainty of two people not yet accustomed to each other. In the process of settling down all lovers become more or less aware of the difference between their conception of their 'love', and what is actually happening to them. Most experience, too, the alarming sensation of the loved person suddenly seeming a total stranger, through the appearance of some unexpected though not necessarily uncongenial aspect of their identity. Any question of identity would be likely to puzzle Othello and throw him off his balance. And there is a difference of identity here which in terms of dramatic poetry is conveyed by the Desdemona of the glove speech, and the Desdemona who proclaimed her love to the senate: it is only the former that Othello knows and loves, but in time he will be able to bridge the gap between the two. Desdemona is unaware of the gap, but her love has a natural resilience which will help to overcome Othello's sense of it. Though she assumes that her lover, to whom she feels so close and with whom she identifies herself completely, will at once see her point about Cassio, she effortlessly modifies this assumption and re-identifies herself with Othello's 'fancies'. She makes the adjustment and goes off quite blithely. But Othello is profoundly shaken. And it is at this moment that Iago, the self-appointed expert in identity, makes his attack. Preoccupied as he is, Othello does not attend for a moment. 'What dost thou say, Iago?' He is not thinking of Cassio but of Desdemona, groping for his sublime image of her – 'one whole, entire, and perfect chrysolite' – and painfully aware of the confusion of the image, as if a stone had scattered a clear reflection. The actor should convey this at a moment of nullity and stasis, a dead spot in love. It is negative, unmeaning, without response or coherence, the 'chaos' which Othello fears. Persons of more emotional experience would know that the mechanism does indeed become inert in this way, for trivial reasons and for short periods, but it is Othello's first taste of such a breakdown. For a man who needs decisiveness so much, the danger of this state is that any suggested cause for it will be eagerly grasped.

This obsession with cause and reason is an ironic aspect of the incomprehension that haunts the play. The word takes on a deep and moving significance at the moment when Othello advances to the act of murder.

> *It is the cause, it is the cause, my soul,*
> *Let me not name it to you, you chaste stars! –*
> *It is the cause.*

The word seems to hypnotize him, and it is difficult not to feel that he clings to it almost as he once clung to his vision of Desdemona. It gives him a vision of universal connection and necessity, and both visions supply his nature with the grounds for action. 'Yet she must die, else she'll betray more men.' His attitude to the adultery is as visionary and as romantic as his former attitude to Desdemona herself. He needs to be certain of it, as he once needed to be certain of his love-vision of her. 'To be once in doubt is once to be resolved.' Doubt is not the lover's state of mind. And it is not the doubting person who is uncomprehending, but the person who must be sure of himself and others: it is no paradox to say that the absence of *doubt* in Othello produces its essential atmosphere of incomprehension and unreality. Othello is torn between his passion for causes and certainties and his natural scope and freedom of impulse, a division that corresponds to the nature of sexual love as at once a prison and a liberation. Othello still voices the claims of scope and freedom even as he demands the proofs of Desdemona's guilt. 'Give me a *living* reason she's disloyal!' Hemmed in as he is by the deadness of causation and analysis – (Iago's analysis of Desdemona's character for example) – he still struggles impossibly to apprehend this dead material in terms of the living dynamism of love.

The attempt is sublimely unreal and a contradiction of great pathos. Yet it manifests his nobility, a nobility quite absent in Leontes of *The Winter's Tale,* who has the same obsession with 'the cause' which has driven him into a state of almost psychopathic unreality. Leontes tries to get rid of the thing by killing his queen, regretting that he cannot kill Polixenes – the other 'part of the cause' – too.

> *– say that she were gone,*
> *Given to the fire, a moiety of my rest*
> *Might come to me again.*

His attitude is on the most elementary moral level; he wants to get rid of the horror and go back – so far as he can – to what he was. But for Othello the cause *is* Desdemona; it is on the same plane as his love for her and must be embraced as absolutely as that love. He could not push her outside himself and return to his former being. And yet he cannot say to Desdemona, like Cordelia to her father – 'no cause, no cause' – because he has confounded cause and reason with the very substance of his love. Love is now dependent on a deluded reason and serves as its liturgy. Of course, reason is a part of love, as Cordelia flatly points out in the opening scene of *Lear,* and as Othello himself would have found in time in his marriage to Desdemona. Love, as

Cordelia knows, comes before reason, though its path should be smoothed and controlled by reason. But Othello can neither renounce love because of reason or discount reason because of love. He must have it both ways. He must have his convictions, however dreadful they are, and his love as well.

... The identity question hangs in the air; Othello is distressed by the momentary disappearance of his image of Desdemona – which has vanished in the actuality of her domestic aplomb and in her introduction of the unfortunate Cassio topic – and it is at this moment that Iago raises the question of what Cassio is *really* like. The world of speculation thus revealed is deeply distasteful to Othello, but it coincides with the disturbance of his vision of Desdemona, a vision which he took for granted with the same sureness and simplicity which he extended to everyone he met. Instead of rejecting this new world out of hand, therefore, Othello listens fascinated to Iago's version of Cassio, the more intently because – as we have seen – conviction of any sort is fatally more acceptable to him than uncertainty. He prefers 'cause' and 'reason' to the withdrawal of emotional initiative and the infliction of mere unease, nullity, emotional slack water. Moreover Iago's comments, with their man of the world air, are impressively specious.

> *But he that filches from me my good name*
> *Robs me of that which not enriches him*
> *And makes me poor indeed.*

That they *are* specious, even at their most sagely generalized, appears in the fact that Iago does indeed hope to be enriched by stealing Cassio's good name: he will get Cassio's job as well as influence over Othello. There is the same air of judicial dispassion in his comment on jealousy – the candid friend concealing nothing but the pleasure he obtains from the effect of his candour.

O beware, my lord, of jealousy;
*It is the green-eyed monster which doth mock**
The meat it feeds on.

The definition horribly fits Iago himself and his own attitude to love, the meat that he mocks and feeds on. In view of the support given by Dr Leavis and others to the view that Iago talks excellent and down-to-earth good sense at times, it is worth restressing the actual disingenuousness of everything he says. It comes out naturalistically in these commonplaces, as it does conventionally in the two-faced oath 'By Janus', and underlines the tragic theme of misunderstanding and incomprehension. Iago equates his cynicism with understanding, but as Conrad remarks in *Chance,* to be without illusions is not the same as to be reasonable. Iago's pseudo-sage comments reflect a kind of infernal muddle between his own desires and his conviction that he alone sees the world steadily and whole.

But his pretension to omniscience is enough to bewilder and corrupt Othello, and his exhibition of the analytic habit implies that it comes naturally to most people, e.g. to Cassio and Desdemona. Othello is made to feel isolated in an idiom totally different from theirs. Yet he returns a typical and spirited reply to Iago's remarks about jealousy.

Think'st thou I'd make a life of jealousy
To follow still the changes of the moon
With fresh suspicions? No! to be once in doubt
Is once to be resolved: exchange me for a goat
When I shall turn the business of my soul
To such exsufflicate and blown surmises
Matching thy inference!

He resists passionately the proffered entertainment which is indeed the 'business' of Iago's soul. His whole

* The suggested emendation of *mock* to *make* is quite unnecessary and weakens the force of the passage.

nature rises to this challenge as it has risen to every other – such a response is almost comfortingly habitual. But he is not to feel this comfort for long. His reply determines Iago to launch his boldest stroke, the climax of his attack: the placing of Desdemona as a typical Venetian girl. It is a risk but it comes off. 'Dost thou say so?' Fascinated and appalled, Othello struggles to adjust himself to this new way of looking at people, catching now at something he has heard Desdemona's father say, and applying it to his own shaken conviction.

I do not think but Desdemona's honest . . .
And yet, how nature erring from itself –

The hesitating cliché is at once taken up, but to show Othello that he is still congenitally out of things, though he has begun to use the jargon of 'knowing', Iago deliberately misunderstands him and gives *nature* his own meaning.

– Ay there's the point: as – to be bold with you –
Not to affect many proposed matches
Of her own clime, complexion, and degree,
Whereto we see all things in nature tends –
Foh! one may smell in such a will most rank,
Foul disproportion, thoughts unnatural.
But pardon me, I do not in position
Distinctly speak of her, though I may fear
Her will, recoiling to her better judgement,
May fail to match you with her country forms
And happily repent.

Othello assumes that it is Desdemona's nature to be honest (i.e. chaste) and that a lapse from this would be unnatural in her; Iago, echoing Brabantio's

For nature so preposterously to err
Sans witchcraft could not –

implies that to the worldly eye the opposite is the case: *nature* determines Desdemona's position as a Venetian girl, with all that that involves. And he gives the concept a further twist by suggesting that Desdemona has shown a viciousness over and above what might be expected of 'our country disposition', by giving way to an unnatural passion for Othello.

These different senses of *nature* may remind us of *King Lear,* where the king assumes that it is on the side of royalty and lawful paternity while Edmund more logically claims its authority for the amoral outlook of the natural son. But there is an illuminating difference. Nature in *Lear* is vast and mysterious, a cloudy spirit which could only manifest itself in poetic drama. In *Othello* it is a word which discloses different attitudes to life, and the misunderstanding and incomprehension which arise from them. Once again the novel lifts its head, in fact, and we shall find that in *The Golden Bowl* the same sort of use is made of different word interpretations, both deliberate and unconscious. For although, as we have seen, Shakespeare drastically modified Cinthio's *novella* in the direction of drama – even dramatic opera – he also transformed and elaborated the implications of the *novella,* and the most notable *donnée* embedded in Cinthio is the corruption of one man's vision of life by another's. Othello is corrupted by Iago's intellectual outlook, and by the logic of knowing and placing, before he is betrayed by the logic of evidence. If he had stayed true to his own nature he would have killed Iago on the spot, as he once slew the 'turbaned Turk': as it is, horror and fascination paralyse him and seduce him into the Iago consciousness. From this moment he is a lost man.

After Iago has gone, the corrupted Othello tries to make use of his wisdom and his 'learned spirit' to rationalize his own situation.

'tis the plague of great ones.
Prerogatived are they less than the base;
'Tis destiny unshunnable, like death:

Even then this forked plague is fated to us
When we do quicken.

There is a subtle piteousness about this which is rare in the drama, rare enough even in the novel, since the novel can hardly command such a merging of the operatic and the realistic. Othello is trying to see his supposed fate as something inevitable for men in his position, and to see it with the worldly calm of an Iago whom nothing puzzles or surprises. Yet he cannot help bringing to the Iago vision a certain ghastly appearance of nobility, just as he later brings to it the instinctive values of his old confident and assertive days. But out of their natural setting these values look incongruous, even hypocritical –

Yet she must die, else she'll betray more men.

The world's honour, we feel, cannot be preserved so. The muddle which resolves itself into these liturgies is very like the one which underlies Iago's assured pronouncements – it is indeed the same muddle. Iago has compelled Othello to rationalize in the way that he himself does, although with Othello concepts like truth and honour are, with a horrible irony, used in the same way as Iago's negative convictions about love and human nature. And Iago's triumph is the virtual absorption of Othello that comes from getting him wholly *placed,* for how can one place someone better than by compelling him to act strictly inside one's own chosen field of understanding? The fallen Othello is no mystery to Iago: he is behaving as men should behave if they are to lend support to Iago's view of the world. That – 'she must die else she'll betray more men' – would have given Iago pure joy if he had heard it, confirming as it does his conviction that all men call their lust, love, and their jealous fury, justice. Iago is driven by the need to make men behave as he thinks they do, and Othello, with his air of massive natural distinction, his absolute singleness of being that cannot be categorized or transfixed with a definition, provides him with a compulsive challenge. He cannot relax until he has Othello safely inside the boundaries of his own perception. Then indeed he can proclaim, reversing their relations with a joyous sarcasm that is lost upon his victim. 'I am your own for ever.'

And yet not quite for ever, except in Othello's own estimation. 'That's he that was Othello.' He indeed is convinced that the demi-devil has snared his soul and that he will be eternally damned for what he has done. The fact makes T. S. Eliot's contention that in the final speeches he is 'cheering himself up, seem a trifle uncharitable, to say the least of it. Even Dante would concede that a sinner condemned to everlasting torment is entitled to whatever crumb of comfort he can get by the way. And Othello convinces us that he means what he says, and that he is sure his suicide will cut him off from the last hope of mercy. To ignore this certainty is to ignore the convictions of religion. The past is all that he has, and it is in the past and in the bounty of his remembered self that he escapes from Iago to the freedom of his love for Desdemona, who loved him for the dangers he had passed. It is here that love triumphs – endures rather – for there is nothing unified about it and nothing ideal. As well as in Othello's recollection it has survived and gleamed forth variously and disconnectedly in Desdemona's last moments; in her 'I am very sorry that you are not well'; in the charming heroine-worship of

Whatever shall become of Michael Cassio
He's never anything but your true servant;

In the pungent common sense of Emilia's views on sex equality, and her – 'Who would not make her husband a cuckold to make him a monarch?' – as well as in her passionate defence of Desdemona. All have a quality and scope that cannot be defined in terms outside themselves; and Iago, the supremely uncharitable impulse, the supreme negation of love, can never wholly succeed in bringing them within the field of his own destructive understanding.

SOURCE: *The Characters of Love* (1962).

NOTE

1. KENT: Is this the promised end?
EDGAR: Or image of that horror?
ALBANY: Fall, and cease.

W. H. Auden

THE JOKER IN THE PACK (1963)

Reason is God's gift; but so are the passions.
Reason is as guilty as passion.

J. H. NEWMAN

I

Any consideration of the Tragedy of Othello must be primarily occupied, not with its official hero but with its villain. I cannot think of any other play in which only one character performs personal actions – all the *deeds* are Iago's – and all the others without exception only exhibit behaviour. In marrying each other, Othello and Desdemona have performed a deed, but this took place before the play begins. Nor can I think of another play in which the villain is so completely triumphant: everything Iago sets out to do, he accomplishes – (among his goals, I include his self-destruction). Even Cassio, who survives, is maimed for life.

If *Othello* is a tragedy – and one certainly cannot call it a comedy – it is tragic in a peculiar way. In most tragedies the fall of the hero from glory to misery and death is the work, either of the gods, or of his own freely chosen acts, or, more commonly, a mixture of both. But the fall of Othello is the work of another human being; nothing he says or does originates with himself. In consequence we feel pity for him but no respect; our aesthetic respect is reserved for Iago.

Iago is a wicked man. The wicked man, the stage villain, as a subject of serious dramatic interest does not, so far as I know, appear in the drama of Western Europe before the Elizabethans. In the mystery plays, the wicked characters, like Satan or Herod, are treated comically, but the theme of the triumphant villain cannot be treated comically because the suffering he inflicts is real.

Coleridge's description of Iago's actions as 'motiveless malignancy' applies in some degree to all the Shakespearian villains. The adjective *motiveless* means, firstly, that the tangible gains, if any, are clearly not the principal motive and, secondly, that the motive is not the desire for personal revenge upon another for a personal injury. Iago himself proffers two reasons for wishing to injure Othello and Cassio. He tells Roderigo that, in appointing Cassio to be his lieutenant, Othello has treated him unjustly, in which conversation he talks like the conventional Elizabethan malcontent. In his soliloquies with himself, he refers to his suspicion that both Othello and Cassio have made him a cuckold, and here he talks like the conventional jealous husband who desires revenge. But there are, I believe, insuperable objections to taking these reasons, as some critics have done, at their face value. If one of Iago's goals is to supplant Cassio in the lieutenancy, one can only say that his plot fails for, when Cassio is cashiered, Othello does not appoint Iago in his place. It is true that, in Act III, scene iii, when they swear blood-brotherhood in revenge, Othello concludes with the words

> ... now thou art my lieutenant

to which Iago replies:

> I am your own for ever

but the use of the word *lieutenant* in this context refers, surely, not to a public military rank, but to a private and illegal delegation of authority – the job delegated to Iago is the secret murder of Cassio, and Iago's reply, which is a mocking echo of an earlier line of Othello's, refers to a relation which can never become public. The ambiguity of the word is confirmed by its use in the first line of the scene which immediately follows. Desdemona says

Do you know, sirrah, where the Lieutenant Cassio
lies?

(One should beware of attaching too much significance to Elizabethan typography, but it is worth noting that Othello's *lieutenant* is in lower case and Desdemona's in upper.) As for Iago's jealousy one cannot believe that a seriously jealous man could behave towards his wife as Iago behaves towards Emilia, for the wife of a jealous husband is the first person to suffer. Not only is the relation of Iago and Emilia, as we see it on stage, without emotional tension, but also Emilia openly refers to a rumour of her infidelity as something already disposed of.

Some such squire it was
That turned your wit, the seamy side without
And made you suspect me with the Moor.

At one point Iago states that, in order to revenge himself on Othello, he will not rest till he is even with him, wife for wife, but, in the play, no attempt at Desdemona's seduction is made. Iago does not make an assault on her virtue himself, he does not encourage Cassio to make one, and he even prevents Roderigo from getting anywhere near her.

Finally, one who seriously desires personal revenge desires to reveal himself. The revenger's greatest satisfaction is to be able to tell his victim to his face – 'You thought you were all-powerful and untouchable and could injure me with impunity. Now you see that you were wrong. Perhaps you have forgotten what you did; let me have the pleasure of reminding you.'

When at the end of the play, Othello asks Iago in bewilderment why he has thus ensnared his soul and body, if his real motive were revenge for having been cuckolded or unjustly denied promotion, he could have said so, instead of refusing to explain.

In Act II, scene i, occur seven lines which, taken in isolation, seem to make Iago a seriously jealous man.

Now I do love her too,
Not out of absolute lust (though peradventure
I stand accountant for as great a sin)
But partly led to diet my revenge
For that I do suspect the lusty Moor
Hath leaped into my seat; the thought whereof
Doth like a poisonous mineral gnaw my vitals.

But if spoken by an actor with serious passion, these lines are completely at variance with the rest of the play, including Iago's other lines on the same subject.

And it is thought abroad, that twixt my sheets
He's done my office: I know not if't be true
Yet I, for mere suspicion in that kind,
Will do, as if for surety.

It is not inconceivable, given the speed at which he wrote, that, at some point in the composition of *Othello*, Shakespeare considered making Iago seriously jealous and, like his prototype in Cinthio, a would-be seducer of Desdemona, and that, when he arrived at his final conception of Iago, he overlooked the incompatibility of the *poisonous mineral* and the *wife-for-wife* passages with the rest.

In trying to understand Iago's character one should begin, I believe, by asking why Shakespeare should have gone to the trouble of inventing Roderigo, a character who has no prototype in Cinthio. From a stage director's point of view, Roderigo is a headache. In the first act we learn that Brabantio had forbidden him the house, from which we must conclude that Desdemona had met him and disliked him as much as her father. In the second act, in order that the audience shall know that he has come to Cyprus, Roderigo has to arrive on the same ship as Desdemona, yet she shows no embarrassment in his presence. Indeed, she and everybody else, except Iago, seem unaware of his existence, for Iago is the only person who ever speaks a word to him. Presumably, he has some official position in the army, but we are never told what it is. His entrances and exits are those of a puppet: whenever Iago has company, he obligingly disappears, and whenever Iago is alone and wishes to speak to him, he comes in again immediately.

Moreover, so far as Iago's plot is concerned, there is nothing Roderigo does which Iago could not do better without him. He could easily have found another means, like an anonymous letter, of informing Brabantio of Desdemona's elopement and, for picking a quarrel with a drunken Cassio, he has, on his own admission, other means handy.

> Three lads of Cyprus, noble swelling spirits
> That hold their honour in a wary distance,
> The very elements of this warlike isle
> Have I to-night flustered with flowing cups.

Since Othello has expressly ordered him to kill Cassio, Iago could have murdered him without fear of legal investigation. Instead, he not only chooses as an accomplice a man whom he is cheating and whose suspicions he has constantly to allay, but also a man who is plainly inefficient as a murderer and also holds incriminating evidence against him.

A man who is seriously bent on revenge does not take unnecessary risks nor confide in anyone whom he cannot trust or do without. Emilia is not, as in Cinthio, Iago's willing accomplice, so that, in asking her to steal the handkerchief, Iago is running a risk, but it is a risk he has to take. By involving Roderigo in his plot, he makes discovery and his own ruin almost certain. It is a law of drama that, by the final curtain, all secrets, guilty or innocent, shall have been revealed so that all, on both sides of the footlights, know who did or did not do what, but usually the guilty are exposed either because, like Edmund, they repent and confess or because of events which they could not reasonably have foreseen. Don John could not have foreseen that Dogberry and Verges would overhear Borachio's conversation, nor Iachimo that Pisanio would disobey Posthumus' order to kill Imogen, nor King Claudius the intervention of a ghost.

Had he wished, Shakespeare could easily have contrived a similar kind of exposure for Iago. Instead, by giving Roderigo the role he does, he makes Iago as a plotter someone devoid of ordinary worldly common sense.

One of Shakespeare's intentions was, I believe, to indicate that Iago desires self-destruction as much as he desires the destruction of others but, before elaborating on this, let us consider Iago's treatment of Roderigo, against whom he has no grievance – it is he who is injuring Roderigo – as a clue to his treatment of Othello and Cassio.

When we first see Iago and Roderigo together, the situation is like that in a Ben Jonson comedy – a clever rascal is gulling a rich fool who deserves to be gulled because his desire is no more moral than that of the more intelligent avowed rogue who cheats him out of his money. Were the play a comedy, Roderigo would finally realize that he had been cheated but would not dare appeal to the law because, if the whole truth were made public, he would cut a ridiculous or shameful figure. But, as the play proceeds, it becomes clear that Iago is not simply after Roderigo's money, a rational motive, but that his main game is Roderigo's moral corruption, which is irrational because Roderigo has given him no cause to desire his moral ruin. When the play opens, Roderigo is shown as a spoiled weakling, but no worse. It may be foolish of him to hope to win Desdemona's affection by gifts and to employ a go-between, but his conduct is not in itself immoral. Nor is he, like Cloten in *Cymbeline,* a brute who regards women as mere objects of lust. He is genuinely shocked as well as disappointed when he learns of Desdemona's marriage, but continues to admire her as a woman full of most blessed condition. Left to himself, he would have had a good bawl, and given her up. But Iago will not let him alone. By insisting that Desdemona is seducible and that his real rival is not Othello but Cassio, he brings Roderigo to entertain the idea, originally foreign to him, of becoming a seducer and of helping Iago to ruin Cassio. Iago had had the pleasure of making a timid conventional man become aggressive and criminal. Cassio beats up Roderigo. Again, at this point, had he been left to himself, he would have gone no further, but Iago will not let him alone until he consents to murder Cassio, a deed which is contrary to his nature, for he is not only timid but also incapable of passionate hatred.

> I have no great devotion to the deed:
> And yet he has given me satisfying reasons.
> 'Tis but a man gone.

Why should Iago want to do this to Roderigo? To me, the clue to this and to all Iago's conduct is to be found in Emilia's comment when she picks up the handkerchief.

> My wayward husband hath a hundred times
> Wooed me to steal it . . .
> what he'll do with it
> Heaven knows, not I,
> I nothing but to please his fantasy.

As his wife, Emilia must know Iago better than anybody else does. She does not know, any more than the others, that he is malevolent, but she does know that her husband is addicted to practical jokes. What Shakespeare gives us in Iago is a portrait of a practical joker of a peculiarly appalling kind, and perhaps the best way of approaching the play is by a general consideration of the Practical Joker.

II

Social relations, as distinct from the brotherhood of a community, are only possible if there is a common social agreement as to which actions or words are to be regarded as serious means to a rational end and which are to be regarded as play, as ends in themselves. In our culture, for example, a policeman must be able to distinguish between a murderous street fight and a boxing match, or a listener between a radio play in which war is declared and a radio news-broadcast announcing a declaration of war.

Social life also presupposes that we may believe what we are told unless we have reason to suppose, either that our informant has a serious motive for deceiving us, or that he is mad and incapable himself of distinguishing between truth and falsehood. If a stranger tries to sell me shares in a gold mine, I shall be a fool if I do not check up on his statements before parting with my money, and if another tells me that he has talked with little men who came out of a flying saucer, I shall assume that he is crazy. But if I ask a stranger the way to the station, I shall assume that his answer is truthful to the best of his knowledge, because I cannot imagine what motive he could have for misdirecting me.

Practical jokes are a demonstration that the distinction between seriousness and play is not a law of nature but a social convention which can be broken, and that a man does not always require a serious motive for deceiving another.

Two men, dressed as city employees, block off a busy street and start digging it up. The traffic cops, motorists and pedestrians assume that this familiar scene has a practical explanation – a water main or an electric cable is being repaired – and make no attempt to use the street. In fact, however, the two diggers are private citizens in disguise who have no business there.

All practical jokes are anti-social acts, but this does not necessarily mean that all practical jokes are immoral. A moral practical joke exposes some flaw in society which is a hindrance to a real community or brotherhood. That it should be possible for two private individuals to dig up a street without being stopped is a just criticism of the impersonal life of a large city where most people are strangers to each other, not brothers; in a village where all the inhabitants know each other personally, the deception would be impossible.

A real community, as distinct from social life, is only possible between persons whose idea of themselves and others is real, not fantastic. There is, therefore, another class of practical jokes which is aimed at particular individuals with the reformatory intent of de-intoxicating them from their illusions. This kind of joke is one of the stock devices of comedy. The deceptions practised on Falstaff by Mistress Page, Mistress Ford and Dame Quickly, or by Octavian on Baron Ochs are possible because these two gentlemen have a fantastic idea of themselves as lady-charmers; the result of the jokes played upon them is that they are brought to a state of self-knowledge and this brings mutual forgiveness and true brotherhood. Similarly, the mock deaths of Hero and of Hermione are ways of bringing home to Claudio and to Leontes how badly they have behaved and of testing the genuineness of their repentance.

All practical jokes, friendly, harmless or malevolent, involve deception, but not all deceptions are practical jokes. The two men digging up the street, for example, might have been two burglars who wished to recover some swag which they knew to be buried there. But, in that case, having found what they were looking for, they would have departed quietly and never been heard of again, whereas, if they are practical jokers, they must reveal afterwards what they have done or the joke will be lost. The practical joker must not only deceive but also, when he has succeeded, unmask and reveal the truth to his victims. The satisfaction of the practical joker is the look of astonishment on the faces of others when they learn that all the time they were convinced that they were thinking and acting on their own initiative, they were actually the puppets of another's will. Thus, though his jokes may be harmless in themselves and extremely funny, there is something slightly sinister about every practical joker, for they betray him as someone who likes to play God behind the scenes. Unlike the ordinary ambitious man who strives for a dominant position in public and enjoys giving orders and seeing others obey them, the practical joker desires to make others obey him without being aware of his existence until the moment of his theophany when he says: 'Behold the God whose puppets you have been and behold, he does not look like a god but is a human being just like yourselves.' The success of a practical joker depends upon his accurate estimate of the weaknesses of others, their ignorances, their social reflexes, their unquestioned presuppositions, their obsessive desires, and even the most harmless practical joke is an expression of the joker's contempt for those he deceives.

But, in most cases, behind the joker's contempt for others lies something else, a feeling of self-insufficiency, of a self lacking in authentic feelings and desires of its own. The normal human being may have a fantastic notion of himself, but he believes in it; he thinks he knows who he is and what he wants so that he demands recognition by others of the value he puts upon himself and must inform others of what he desires if they are to satisfy them.

But the self of the practical joker is unrelated to his joke. He manipulates others but, when he finally reveals his identity, his victims learn nothing about his nature, only something about their own; they know how it was possible for them to be decieved but not why he chose to deceive them. The only answer that any practical joker can give to the question: 'Why did you do this?' is Iago's: 'Demand me nothing. What you know, you know.'

In fooling others, it cannot be said that the practical joker satisfies any concrete desire of his nature; he has only demonstrated the weaknesses of others and all he can now do, once he has revealed his existence, is to bow and retire from the stage. He is only related to others, that is, so long as they are unaware of his existence; once they are made aware of it, he cannot fool them again, and the relation is broken off.

The practical joker despises his victims, but at the same time he envies them because their desires, however childish and mistaken, are real to them, whereas he has no desire which he can call his own. His goal, to make game of others, makes his existence absolutely dependent upon theirs; when he is alone, he is a nullity. Iago's self-description, *I am not what I am,* is correct and the negation of the Divine *I am that I am.* If the word motive is given its normal meaning of a positive purpose of the self like sex, money, glory, etc., then the practical joker is without motive. Yet the professional practical joker is certainly driven, like a gambler, to his activity, but the drive is negative, a fear of lacking a concrete self, of being nobody. In any practical joker to whom playing such jokes is a passion, there is always an element of malice, a projection of his self-hatred onto others, and in the ultimate case of the absolute practical joker, this is projected onto all created things. Iago's statement, 'I am not what I am,' is given its proper explanation in the *Credo* which Boito wrote for him in his libretto for Verdi's opera.

Credo in un Dio crudel che m'ha creato
Simile a se, e che nell'ira io nomo.
Dall viltà d'un germe e d'un atomo
Vile son nato,
Son scellerato
Perchè son uomo:
E sento il fango originario in me
E credo l'uom gioco d'iniqua sorte
Dal germe della culla
Al verme dell'avel.
Vien dopo tanto irrision la Morte
E poi? La Morte e il Nulla.

Equally applicable to Iago is Valéry's 'Ebauche d'un serpent.' The serpent speaks to God the Creator thus

O Vanité! Cause Première
Celui qui règne dans les Cieux

D'une voix qui fut la lumière
Ouvrit l'univers spacieux.
Comme las de son pur spectacle
Dieu lui-même a rompu l'obstacle
De sa parfaite éternité;
Il se fit Celui qui dissipe
En conséquences son Principe,
En étoiles son Unité.

And of himself thus

Je suis Celui qui modifie,

the ideal motto, surely, for Iago's coat of arms.

Since the ultimate goal of Iago is nothingness, he must not only destroy others, but himself as well. Once Othello and Desdemona are dead his 'occupation's gone.'

To convey this to an audience demands of the actor who plays the role the most violent contrast in the way he acts when Iago is with others and the way he acts when he is left alone. With others, he must display every virtuoso trick of dramatic technique for which great actors are praised, perfect control of movement, gesture, expression, diction, melody and timing, and the ability to play every kind of role, for there are as many 'honest' Iagos as there are characters with whom he speaks, a Roderigo Iago, a Cassio Iago, an Othello Iago, a Desdemona Iago, etc. When he is alone, on the other hand, the actor must display every technical fault for which bad actors are criticized. He must deprive himself of all stage presence, and he must deliver the lines of his soliloquies in such a way that he makes nonsense of them. His voice must lack expression, his delivery must be atrocious, he must pause where the verse calls for no pauses, accentuate unimportant words, etc.

III

If Iago is so alienated from nature and society that he has no relation to time and place – he could turn up anywhere at any time – his victims are citizens of Shakespeare's Venice. To be of dramatic interest, a character must to some degree be at odds with the society of which he is a member, but his estrangement is normally an estrangement from a specific social situation.

Shakespeare's Venice is a mercantile society, the purpose of which is not military glory but the acquisition of wealth. However, human nature being what it is, like any other society, it has enemies, trade rivals, pirates, etc., against whom it must defend itself, if necessary by force. Since a mercantile society regards warfare as a disagreeable, but unfortunately sometimes unavoidable, activity and not, like a feudal aristocracy, as a form of play, it replaces the old feudal levy by a paid professional army, nonpolitical employees of the State, to whom fighting is their specialized job.

In a professional army, a soldier's military rank is not determined by his social status as a civilian, but by his military efficiency. Unlike the feudal knight who has a civilian home from which he is absent from time to time but to which, between campaigns, he regularly returns, the home of the professional soldier is an army camp and he must go wherever the State sends him. Othello's account of his life as a soldier, passed in exotic landscapes and climates, would have struck Hotspur as unnatural, unchivalrous and no fun.

A professional army has its own experiences and its own code of values which are different from those of civilians. In *Othello*, we are shown two societies, that of the city of Venice proper and that of the Venetian army. The only character who, because he is equally estranged from both, can simulate being equally at home in both, is Iago. With army folk he can play the blunt soldier, but in his first scene with Desdemona upon their arrival in Cyprus, he speaks like a character out of *Love's Labour's Lost*. Cassio's comment.

> Madam, you may relish him more in the soldier than
> the scholar

is provoked by envy. Iago has excelled him in the euphuistic flirtatious style of conversation which he considers his forte. Roderigo does not feel at home, either with civilians or with soldiers. He lacks the charm which makes a man a success with the ladies, and the physical courage and heartiness which make a man popular in an army mess. The sympathetic aspect of his character, until Iago destroys it, is a certain humility; he knows that he is a person of no consequence. But for Iago, he would have remained a sort of Bertie Wooster, and one suspects that the notion that Desdemona's heart might be softened by expensive presents was not his own but suggested to him by Iago.

In deceiving Roderigo, Iago has to overcome his consciousness of his inadequacy, to persuade him that he could be what he knows he is not, charming, brave, successful. Consequently, to Roderigo and, I think, to Roderigo only, Iago tells direct lies. The lie may be on a point of fact, as when he tells Roderigo that Othello and Desdemona are not returning to Venice but going to Mauritania, or a lie about the future, for it is obvious that, even if Desdemona is seducible, Roderigo will never be the man. I am inclined to think that the story Iago tells Roderigo about his disappointment over the lieutenancy is a deliberate fabrication. One notices, for example, that he contradicts himself. At first he claims that Othello had appointed Cassio in spite of the request of three great ones of the city who had recommended Iago, but then a few lines later, he says

> Preferment goes by letter and affection,
> Not by the old gradation where each second
> Stood heir to the first.

In deceiving Cassio and Othello, on the other hand, Iago has to deal with characters who consciously think well of themselves but are unconsciously insecure. With them, therefore, his tactics are different; what he says to them is always possibly true.

...Cassio is a ladies' man, not a seducer. With women of his own class, what he enjoys is socialized eroticism; he would be frightened of a serious personal passion. For physical sex he goes to prostitutes and when, unexpectedly, Bianca falls in love with him, like many of his kind, he behaves like a cad and brags of his conquest to others. Though he does not know who the owner of the handkerchief actually is, he certainly knows that Bianca will think that it belongs to another woman, and to ask her to copy it is gratuitous cruelty. His smiles, gestures and remarks about Bianca to Iago are insufferable in themselves; to Othello, who knows that he is talking about a woman, though he is mistaken as to her identity, they are an insult which only Cassio's death can avenge.

In Cinthio nothing is said about the Moor's colour or religion, but Shakespeare has made Othello a black Negro who has been baptized.

No doubt there are differences between colour prejudice in the twentieth century and colour prejudice in the seventeenth and probably few of Shakespeare's audience had ever seen a Negro, but the slave trade was already flourishing and the Elizabethans were certainly no innocents to whom a Negro was simply a comic exotic. Lines like

> ...an old black ram
> is tupping your white ewe...
> The gross clasps of a lascivious Moor...
> What delight shall she have to look on the devil

are evidence that the paranoid fantasies of the white man in which the Negro appears as someone who is at one and the same time less capable of self-control and more sexually potent than himself, fantasies with which, alas, we are only too familiar, already were rampant in Shakespeare's time.

The Venice of both *The Merchant of Venice* and *Othello* is a cosmopolitan society in which there are two kinds of social bond between its members, the bond of economic interest and the bond of personal friendship, which may coincide, run parallel with each other or conflict, and both plays are concerned with an extreme case of conflict.

Venice needs financiers to provide capital and it needs the best general it can hire to defend it; it so happens that the most skilful financier it can find is a Jew and the best general a Negro, neither of whom the majority are willing to accept as a brother.

Though both are regarded as outsiders by the Venetian community, Othello's relation to it differs from Shylock's. In the first place, Shylock rejects the Gentile community as firmly as the Gentile community rejects him; he is just as angry when he hears that Jessica has married Lorenzo as Brabantio is about Desdemona's elopement with Othello. In the second place, while the profession of usurer, however socially useful, is regarded as ignoble, the military profession, even though the goal of a mercantile society is not military glory, is still highly admired and, in addition, for the sedentary civilians who govern the city, it has a romantic exotic glamour which it cannot have in a feudal society in which fighting is a familiar shared experience.

Thus no Venetian would dream of spitting on Othello and, so long as there is no question of his marrying into the family, Brabantio is delighted to entertain the famous general and listen to his stories of military life. In the army, Othello is accustomed to being obeyed and treated with the respect due to his rank and, on his rare visits to the city, he is treated by the white aristocracy as someone important and interesting. Outwardly, nobody treats him as an outsider as they treat Shylock. Consequently, it is easy for him to persuade himself that he is accepted as a brother and when Desdemona accepts him as a husband, he seems to have proof of this.

It is painful to hear him say

> But that I love the gentle Desdemona
> I would not my unhoused free condition
> Put into circumscription or confine
> For the sea's worth

for the condition of the outsider is always unhoused and free. He does not or will not recognize that Brabantio's view of the match

> If such actions may have passage free,
> Bond-slaves and pagans shall our statesmen be

is shared by all his fellow senators, and the arrival of news about the Turkish fleet prevents their saying so because their need of Othello's military skill is too urgent for them to risk offending him.

If one compares *Othello* with the other plays in which Shakespeare treats the subject of male jealousy, *The Winter's Tale* and *Cymbeline,* one notices that Othello's jealousy is of a peculiar kind.

Leontes is a classical case of paranoid sexual jealousy due to repressed homosexual feelings. He has absolutely no evidence that Hermione and Polixenes have committed adultery and his entire court are convinced of their innocence, but he is utterly possessed by his fantasy. As he says to Hermione: 'Your actions are my dream.' But, mad as he is, 'the twice-nine changes of the Watery Starre' which Polixenes has spent at the Bohemian court, make the act of adultery physically possible so that, once the notion has entered his head, neither Hermione nor Polixenes nor the court can prove that it is false. Hence the appeal to the Oracle.

Posthumus is perfectly sane and is convinced against

his will that Imogen has been unfaithful because Iachimo offers him apparently irrefutable evidence that adultery has taken place.

But both the mad Leontes and the sane Posthumus react in the same way: 'My wife has been unfaithful; therefore she must be killed and forgotten.' That is to say, it is only as husbands that their lives are affected. As king of Bohemia, as a warrior, they function as if nothing has happened.

In *Othello,* thanks to Iago's manipulations, Cassio and Desdemona behave in a way which would make it not altogether unreasonable for Othello to suspect that they were in love with each other, but the time factor rules out the possibility of adultery having been actually committed. Some critics have taken the double time in the play to be merely a dramaturgical device for speeding the action which the audience in the theatre will never notice. I believe, however, that Shakespeare meant the audience to notice it as, in *The Merchant of Venice,* he meant them to notice the discrepancy between Belmont time and Venice time.

If Othello had simply been jealous of the feelings for Cassio he imagined Desdemona to have, he would have been sane enough, guilty at worst of a lack of trust in his wife. But Othello is not merely jealous of feelings which might exist; he demands proof of an act which could not have taken place, and the effect on him of believing in this physical impossibility goes far beyond wishing to kill her: it is not only his wife who has betrayed him but the whole universe; life has become meaningless, his occupation is gone.

This reaction might be expected if Othello and Desdemona were a pair like Romeo and Juliet or Antony and Cleopatra whose love was an all-absorbing Tristan–Isolde kind of passion, but Shakespeare takes care to inform us that it was not.

When Othello asks leave to take Desdemona with him to Cyprus, he stresses the spiritual element in his love.

I therefore beg it not
To please the palate of my appetite
Nor to comply with heat, the young affects
In me defunct, and proper satisfaction,
But to be free and bounteous of her mind.

Though the imagery in which he expresses his jealousy is sexual – what other kind of images could he use? – Othello's marriage is important to him less as a sexual relationship than as a symbol of being loved and accepted as a person, a brother in the Venetian community. The monster in his own mind too hideous to be shown is the fear he has so far repressed that he is only valued for his social usefulness to the City. But for his occupation, he would be treated as a black barbarian.

The overcredulous, overgood-natured character which, as Iago tells us, Othello had always displayed is a telltale symptom. He had *had* to be overcredulous in order to compensate for his repressed suspicions. Both in his happiness at the beginning of the play and in his cosmic despair later, Othello reminds one more of Timon of Athens than of Leontes.

Since what really matters to Othello is that Desdemona should love him as the person he really is, Iago has only to get him to suspect that she does not, to release the repressed fears and resentments of a lifetime, and the question of what she has done or not done is irrelevant.

Iago treats Othello as an analyst treats a patient except that, of course, his intention is to kill not to cure. Everything he says is designed to bring to Othello's consciousness what he has already guessed is there. Accordingly, he has no need to tell lies. Even his speech, 'I lay with Cassio lately,' can be a truthful account of something which actually happened: from what we know of Cassio, he might very well have such a dream as Iago reports. Even when he has worked Othello up to a degree of passion where he would risk nothing by telling a direct lie, his answer is equivocal and its interpretation is left to Othello.

OTHELLO: What hath he said?
IAGO: Faith that he did – I know not what he did.
OTHELLO: But what?
IAGO: Lie——
OTHELLO: With her?
IAGO: With her, on her, what you will.

Nobody can offer Leontes absolute proof that his jealousy is baseless; similarly, as Iago is careful to point out, Othello can have no proof that Desdemona really is the person she seems to be.

...Once Othello allows himself to suspect that Desdemona may not be the person she seems, she cannot allay the suspicion by telling the truth but she can appear to confirm it by telling a lie. Hence the catastrophic effect when she denies having lost the handkerchief.

If Othello cannot trust her, then he can trust nobody and nothing, and precisely what she has done is not important. In the scene where he pretends that the Castle is a brothel of which Emilia is the Madam, he accuses Desdemona, not of adultery with Cassio, but of nameless orgies.

DESDEMONA: Alas, what ignorant sin have I committed?
OTHELLO: Was this fair paper, this most goodly book
Made to write whore on. What committed?
Committed. O thou public commoner,
I should make very forges of my cheeks
That would to cinders burn up modesty
Did I but speak thy deeds.

And, as Mr Eliot has pointed out, in his farewell speech his thoughts are not on Desdemona at all but upon his relation to Venice, and he ends by identifying himself with another outsider, the Moslem Turk who beat a Venetian and traduced the state.

Everybody must pity Desdemona, but I cannot bring myself to like her. Her determination to marry Othello – it was she who virtually did the proposing – seems the romantic crush of a silly schoolgirl rather than a mature affection; it is Othello's adventures, so unlike the civilian life she knows, which captivate her rather than Othello as a person. He may not have practised withcraft, but, in fact, she is spellbound. And despite all Brabantio's prejudices, her deception of her own father makes an unpleasant impression: Shakespeare does not allow us to forget that the shock of the marriage kills him.

Then, she seems more aware than is agreeable of the honour she has done Othello by becoming his wife. When Iago tells Cassio that 'our General's wife is now the General' and, soon afterwards, soliloquizes.

> His soul is so infettered to her love
> That she may make, unmake, do what she list
> Even as her appetite shall play the god
> With his weak function,

he is, no doubt, exaggerating, but there is much truth in what he says. Before Cassio speaks to her, she has already discussed him with her husband and learned that he is to be reinstated as soon as is opportune. A sensible wife would have told Cassio this and left matters alone. In continuing to badger Othello, she betrays a desire to prove to herself and to Cassio that she can make her husband do as she pleases.

Her lie about the handkerchief is, in itself, a trivial fib but, had she really regarded her husband as her equal, she might have admitted the loss. As it is, she is frightened because she is suddenly confronted with a man whose sensibility and superstitions are alien to her.

Though her relation with Cassio is perfectly innocent, one cannot but share Iago's doubts as to the durability of the marriage. It is worth noting that, in the willow-song scene with Emilia, she speaks with admiration of Lodovico and then turns to the topic of adultery. Of course, she discusses this in general terms and is shocked by Emilia's attitude, but she does discuss the subject and she does listen to what Emilia has to say about husbands and wives. It is as if she had suddenly realized that she had made a *mésalliance* and that the sort of man she ought to have married was someone of her own class and colour like Lodovico. Given a few more years of Othello and of Emilia's influence and she might well, one feels, have taken a lover.

IV

And so one comes back to where one started, to Iago, the sole agent in the play. A play, as Shakespeare said, is a mirror held up to nature. This particular mirror bears the date 1604, but, when we look into it, the face that confronts us is our own in the middle of the twentieth century. We hear Iago say the same words and see him do the same things as an Elizabethan audience heard and saw, but what they mean to us cannot be exactly the same. To his first audience and even, maybe, to his creator, Iago appeared to be just another Machiavellian villain who might exist in real life but with whom one would never dream of identifying oneself. To us, I think, he is a much more alarming figure; we cannot hiss at him when he appears as we can hiss at the villain in a Western movie because none of us can honestly say that he does not understand how such a wicked person can exist. For is not Iago, the practical joker, a parabolic figure for the autonomous pursuit of scientific knowledge through experiment which we all, whether we are scientists or not, take for granted as natural and right?

As Nietzsche said, experimental science is the last flower of asceticism. The investigator must discard all his feelings, hopes and fears as a human person and reduce himself to a disembodied observer of events upon which he passes no value judgment. Iago is an ascetic. 'Love' he says, 'is merely a lust of the blood, and a permission of the will.'

The knowledge sought by science is only one kind of knowledge. Another kind is that implied by the Biblical phrase, 'Then Adam knew Eve, his wife,' and it is this kind I still mean when I say, 'I know John Smith very well.' I cannot know in this sense without being known in return. If I know John Smith well, he must also know me well.

But, in the scientific sense of knowledge, I can only know that which does not and cannot know me. Feeling unwell, I go to my doctor who examines me, says 'You have Asian flu,' and gives me an injection. The Asian virus is as unaware of my doctor's existence as his victims are of a practical joker.

Further, to-know in the scientific sense means, ultimately, to-have-power-over. To the degree that human beings are authentic persons, unique and self-creating, they cannot be scientifically known. But human beings are not pure persons like angels; they are also biological organisms, almost identical in their functioning, and, to a greater or lesser degree, they are neurotic, that is to say, less free than they imagine because of fears and desires of which they have no personal knowledge but could and ought to have. Hence, it is always possible to reduce human beings to the status of things which are completely scientifically knowable and completely controllable.

This can be done by direct action on their bodies with drugs, lobotomies, deprivation of sleep, etc. The difficulty about this method is that your victims will know that you are trying to enslave them and, since nobody wishes to be a slave, they will object, so that it can only be practised upon minorities like prisoners and lunatics who are physically incapable of resisting.

The other method is to play on the fears and desires of which you are aware and they are not until they enslave themselves. In this case, concealment of your real intention is not only possible but essential for, if people know they are being played upon, they will not believe what you say or do what you suggest. An advertisement based on snob appeal, for example, can only succeed with people who are unaware that they are snobs and that their snobbish feelings are being appealed to and to whom, therefore, your advertisement seems as honest as Iago seems to Othello.

Iago's treatment of Othello conforms to Bacon's definition of scientific enquiry as putting Nature to the Question. If a member of the audience were to interrupt the play and ask him: 'What are you doing?' could not Iago answer with a boyish giggle, 'Nothing. I'm only trying to find out what Othello is really like'? And we must admit that his experiment is highly successful. By the end of the play he does know the scientific truth about the object to which he has reduced Othello. That is what makes his parting shot, 'What you know, you know,' so terrifying for, by then, Othello has become a thing, incapable of knowing anything.

And why shouldn't Iago do this? After all, he has certainly acquired knowledge. What makes it impossible for us to condemn him self-righteously is that, in our culture, we have all accepted the notion that the right to know is absolute and unlimited. The gossip column is one side of the medal; the cobalt bomb the other. We are quite prepared to admit that, while food and sex are good in themselves, an uncontrolled pursuit of either is not, but it is difficult for us to believe that intellectual curiosity is a desire like any other, and to realize that correct knowledge and truth are not identical. To apply a categorical imperative to knowing, so that, instead of asking, 'What can I know?' we ask, 'What, at this moment, am I meant to know?' – to entertain the possibility that the only knowledge which can be true for us is the knowledge we can live up to – that seems to all of us crazy and almost immoral. But, in that case, who are we to say to Iago – 'No, you mustn't.'

SOURCE: *The Dyer's Hand* (1963).

Nevill Coghill

FROM *SHAKESPEARE'S PROFESSIONAL SKILLS* (1964)

FROM THE PREFACE: INTERPRETATION AND THE 'DISCIPLINE OF THE THEATRE'

...I say it is extremely difficult and tiring, when reading a play, to hold it in the mind's eye, and in the mind's ear, with any constancy, as it moves from moment to moment. It asks more concentration than most of us have to remember (for instance) while we are reading, what characters are on the stage, in what costumes and attitudes. The less we can do this, the more we are likely to lose important inflections of meaning. In a small scene, such as that between the Old Countess and Helena in the first act of *All's Well that Ends Well*, we may be able to visualise the two figures, both in their mourning black, each with her special grace – the graces of age and nobility and the grace of youth in love – the Countess seated, perhaps, with Helena kneeling at her side, and see their gestures and expressions, hear the tones of their talk as they flow through the dialogue, packing it with live meaning. But with more complex scenes, who can hold all their detail for long in his imagination, as the moods and movements change, while he reads?

It is false to reply that such visual details cannot carry important significances, as we shall soon see. The Elizabethans were certainly alive to some of them; they had whole systems of colour-symbolism in dress for instance, and a lover would, by wearing the colours of his mistress, 'carry on a silent conversation or flirtation with her'; it was an elaborate language, highly expressive. The instinct survives; this afternoon

I saw a young man whose hair was dyed and styled to match precisely the dye and style of the hair of his girl-friend; they were walking hand in hand. It gave an effect of meaning that the eye could not miss, but eludes a full expression in words.

But it is generally not from our incapacities to visualise, that our worst distortions of Shakespeare come; it is from the lawlessness of our imaginations that we are in real danger; ingenious fancies, that lack the discipline of theatre, lead us into every kind of licentious speculation, even to wresting anti-Shakespearean meanings from his texts. Those, however, who are seeking Shakespeare's own meanings – an activity that seems legitimate and not entirely hopeless – can teach themselves, at least in some cases, to distinguish between an interpretation that has genuine Shakespearean validity, and one that has it doubtfully, or not at all, by simply seeing if it could work on the stage; if not, it is a private fantasy.

Let us offer a swift example, taken from many years back, though it is still much quoted. In an essay on 'Shakespeare and the Stoicism of Seneca', by Mr T. S. Eliot, first published in 1927, he discusses Othello's last long speech, that begins:

> Soft you; a word or two before you goe: (v ii 341)

This he considers an example of what he calls *Bovarysme* in the Moor; *Bovarysme* he defines as 'the human will to see things as they are not', a thing exemplified (he thinks) in a high degree in these lines, though generations of readers and playgoers have mistakenly thought the speech to express 'the greatness in defeat of a noble but erring nature'.

But Mr Eliot will not allow this consoling view to be the true burden of Othello's speech, for he takes it as that of a man 'endeavouring to escape from reality': Othello has 'ceased to think about Desdemona' to indulge in self-pity; what he is really doing is '*cheering himself up*' for the frightful mess his folly has made.

What happens to this interpretation when we try it out in a theatre? What tones of voice, what move or gesture, can an actor use to suggest a Bovarist cheering himself up? Would he not choose precisely those that would seem to be 'expressing the greatness in defeat of a noble nature'? For a true Bovarist at such a moment would attempt to see himself as doing exactly that. Unless it be argued that there is no such thing in nature as greatness in defeat, and that any attempt to show it must be instantly recognised by all as fraudulent, how is an audience to know whether Othello is cheering himself up for being so gross a fool and failure, or whether he is cheering his audience up by showing once again, and at the last moment, a true flash of that nobility for which they had first honoured him?

The gravamen of the charge against such criticism is not simply that it is foot-loose from the art it is attempting to criticise, but that it implies a shocking technical incompetence, or else a shocking moral irresponsibility, in Shakespeare as a playwright. For if Shakespeare had wished to convey the 'terrible exposure of human weakness' that Mr Eliot sees in Othello's speech, he could very easily have made this simple purpose plain, unless he was a bungler, or quite indifferent to the effect he was creating. For if Mr Eliot is right, the better this speech is spoken and acted, the more it must deceive the audience; and this is, in effect, conceded by Mr Eliot, who says Othello 'takes in the spectator'. It follows then, that what begins as an attack on Othello's character turns out as undermining Shakespeare's craftsmanship. In the pleasures of self-abasement and the denigration of heroism, many have welcomed Mr Eliot's views without noticing where they were leading, all for want of thinking in terms of the medium Shakespeare used.

It is pardonable for a *reader*, under the spell of Othello's speech, to have forgotten, that Iago is still on stage and in full possession of his faculties. His hatred of Othello is undiminished. Had it been Shakespeare's intention to suggest what Mr Eliot supposes, Iago was there to assist him. Shakespeare had endowed him with the capacity to puncture sentiment; we have heard him use it on Roderigo:

> *Rod.* I cannot beleeue that in her, she's full of most bless'd condition.
> *Iago.* Bless'd figges-end. (II i 245–6)

What prevented Shakespeare, if he wished us to think ignobly of Othello's soul, from using Iago to guide our understanding to this crucial point? Iago had only to choose his moment in Othello's speech to ejaculate 'Thicklips!' or 'Buzze buzze!' (since, alas, the more sophisticated '*Bovarist!*' was not then available) to make his point. But the point was not made.

Under the discipline of theatre, then, the whole Bovarist conjecture collapses, like many other critical glosses on Shakespeare that have been offered without considering what can happen on a stage. An art moves in its own medium. Critics, like producers, must feel for the ways in which the plays they discuss were meant to *work*, both as a whole and in points of detail. These ways, or some of them, are the subject of this book.

FROM CHAPTER VI: 'SOLILOQUY'

...In *Othello* there are two soliloquists, Iago and Othello. Iago has eight soliloquies, Othello three. Iago needs this number to reveal, first, the quality of his own tortuous nature and, secondly, the detail of his intentions. Broadly speaking, his first three soliloquies are epiphanies, the last five, signposts.

The three in which he reveals his nature are unique in Shakespeare. Professor Spivak asks: 'Is it not an undeviating practice of the Elizabethan dramaturgy that the soliloquy is an instrument of direct revelation, providing information that the audience need to have and would not otherwise clearly get at all?'[1] The information Iago gives is indeed necessary; but it is information about himself, not about any objective world. When he tells us of Othello that

> it is thought abroad, that 'twixt my sheetes
> Ha's done my office; I know not, if't be true –
> (Q I iii 381–2)

this is not to be taken as evidence that there was a rumour of this kind going about. If Shakespeare had meant us to believe this, nothing would have been easier for him than to make Roderigo or Montano, or even the Clown, blurt it out. But we never hear the slightest hint of it; it is one of Iago's inventions, and gives us clear information about his state of mind; he is not under hallucination, as Macbeth is in his 'dagger-speech'; he is in the subtler, but very common condition, which almost everyone experiences in some degree, of one who is entertaining a fantasy in order to feed a passion.

Psychologically, Iago is a slighted man, powerfully possessed by hatred against a master who (as he thinks) has kept him down, and by envy for a man he despises who has been promoted over him. All this comes out in the first lines of the play. Such a man will naturally have a fantasy life in which he can hate these enemies the more, that he may revenge himself upon them the more. The fantasy that comes most easily to him is that of crude copulation; it is his theme-song. In the opening scene his language to Brabantio is all stallion, and now his first thought is

> to abuse *Othello's* eares,
> That he is too familiar with his wife.
> (F I iii 389–90)

His next idea is to diet his revenge on Desdemona himself, 'not out of absolute lust', as he says; but in order to spite Othello, whom (of course) he now fancies to have 'leap't into his seat' and debauched Emilia. So strong with him is this vulgar fantasy that he extends it to Cassio as well.

> (For I feare *Cassio* with my Night-Cape* too)
> (F II i 301)

He indulges these imaginings as a sadist will conjure up whole histories of imaginary crimes committed by the victim he is about to chain up and whip, so that he may 'punish' them. He may not exactly 'believe' in the imputed guilt, but he pretends to because it gives relish to his performance.

But these elementary things in psychology are not the most important things in Iago's soliloquies. It does not matter very much whether an audience believes that he has really heard the rumours he speaks of, or whether they have fabricated themselves within him to sharpen his pleasure in revenge.

What is more important (as our analysis will show) is that his first three soliloquies are *graded in order of heinousness,* the foulest last. Their function is not to bring him closer to and create sympathy for him in the audience (as in the case of Brutus) but to distance him from them, to create hatred for him. This is what is unique in them. The soliloquies of Richard III, a very different kind of villain and self-revealer, actually win his hearers over to him: just as he wins Anne to be his wife over the dead body of her father-in-law, so he wins the audience (over many other dead bodies) by his fellow-conspirator wit in soliloquy; but Iago's soliloquies are designed to make him progressively more repellent. They are the hairpin bends by which we descend into the abysses of his nature.

Yet there is a third purpose to be discerned in these speeches. They are there to offer the living image of a man who is the opposite of what he appears to be. He is a walking illustration of the theme with which he opens the play:

> I am not what I am. (F I i 66)

* [*read* night-cap]

Just as in the depths of the sea there have been charted great rivers (that make a trickle of the Amazon) which flow in a constant direction in perpetual spate, so in Shakespeare's mind may be tracked certain powerful and constant currents of thought, that flow through many plays; and this is one of them. It breaks surface from time to time among many other themes, and especially perhaps at this period in his life as a writer (between *Hamlet* and *Macbeth*). In no one is it more sharply presented than in Iago, in whom there is no twilight in the night-and-day of his behaviour: the moment we are alone with him, or when he is alone with his dupe Roderigo, his night falls: but when he is seen in any other company he is bright with good fellowship and honest concern for others, as I shall show. By the peculiar use of soliloquy allotted to Iago, Shakespeare sought to give definition to this embodiment of an obsessive theme of his: we see and hear alternately what Iago is and seems.

He begins with no clear plan at all. We are shown him trying treacherously to embroil his master with a senator. It is never told us what he hopes to gain by this, except the satisfaction of a revenge on the Moor for Cassio's promotion. But, for this opportunist, spite is satisfaction enough. Seeing, however, that his own fortunes are dependent upon Othello's, it does not appear that to rouse a senator against the Moor will advance his personal position. He tells Roderigo that he has a 'peculiar end' for his behaviour (I i 61), but this is a fantasy too; his plot against Othello does not become clear to him until much later, when it comes in a flash, in all its monstrous logic, in the third of his graded soliloquies. Let us take them in order.

The first is placed at the end of Act I. The care of Desdemona has just been entrusted to him and he is left with Roderigo, whom he immediately instructs in the means of seducing her. Roderigo, gulled by his hopes and lusts, goes out obediently to sell all his land. It is time for Iago to explain himself a little to the audience. Once again he asserts the basic fact:

I hate the Moore (F I iii 380)

and gives us a first pointer to the plot that is forming in his mind:

Let me see now,
To get his Place, and to plume vp my will
In double Knauery. How? How? Let's see.
After some time, to abuse *Othello*'s eares,
That he is too familiar with his wife...
(F I iii 386–90)

and he finishes this aspect of the soliloquy with

I haue't: it is engendred: Hell, and Night,
Must bring this monstrous Birth, to the world's
light. (F I iii 397–8)

In his second soliloquy, he brings his plot into slightly sharper focus; he will abuse Cassio to the Moor and make the Moor thank him and reward him for 'making him egregiously an Asse': but still the line of action is a little blurred:

'Tis heere: but yet confus'd,
Knaueries plaine face, is neuer seene, till vs'd.
(F II i 305–6)

The complete, explicit plot is reserved for the third soliloquy:

For whiles this honest Foole
Plies *Desdemona* to repair his Fortune,
And she for him, pleades strongly to the Moore,
Ile powre this pestilence into his eare:
That she repeales him, for her bodies Lust.
(F II iii 342–6)

His five other soliloquies are direct signposts about the working of his plots, and their function is to give a practical shape to his thoughts, rather than a psychological. The three soliloquies we have discussed offer us a progressive clarification of his schemes; they also offer a progressive exhibition of the evil in him. Brutus shows us his soul, Iago his brains, a fresh step down at each epiphany. His first motive is factual: he tells Roderigo that he has been passed over for promotion; but his first soliloquy already passes over into the fantasy we have discussed, the inventive mania of a sense of injury, in a man obsessed by sex:

I hate the Moore,
And it is thought abroad, that twixt my sheetes
Ha's done my office: I know not, if't be true –
Yet I, for mere suspition in that kind,
Will doe, as if for surety.... (Q I iii 380–4)

In his first soliloquy he descends from professional jealousy to sexual jealousy; in his second the sexual fantasies begin to proliferate and the sharp pleasure of a revenging copulation begins to rouse in him a kind of lust, leading to the neat, exciting cruelty of

And nothing can, or shall content my Soule
Till I am eeuen'd with him, wife, for wift.*
(F II i 292–3)

But there is worse to come. It is not enough for him to use Desdemona's body against Othello, he means to use her soul. We hear no more about his wanting to enjoy her; that fantasy gives way to the foulest he can think of, with a diabolical theology of its own, which he calls 'Divinity of Hell'.

And by how much she striues to do him good,
She shall vndo her Credite with the Moore.
So will I turne her vertue into pitch,
And out of her owne goodnesse make the Net,
That shall en-mesh them all. (F II iii 347–51)

* [*read* wife]

These three speeches, then, go steadily deeper into a repulsive evil, sauced by a sneering contempt for all that may be thought holy and good. 'Contempt', said Coleridge, 'is never attributed in Shakespeare, but to characters deep in villainy, as Edmund, Iago, Antonio, and Sebastian.'[2]

But Shakespeare is just as careful to show Iago fair in public as he is to show him foul in private. It is this that makes him so detestable, so atrocious in his evil. It is the major strategy of the play, not only that every other character should think him 'honest' but that the audience should see why they do so. Two scenes in particular are planned so as to bring this about. The first is the scene of Desdemona's arrival in Cyprus, and the second is that of the drunken brawl that brings disgrace on Cassio.

Desdemona arrives in the midst of a violent storm; it has separated her from Othello. But why did Shakespeare choose to place them in different ships to begin with, and then invent a storm to part them? Was it to symbolise the inward storm about to break over and separate them till death? Possibly. But there was also a more practical reason. By telling his story in this way he was able to show what a delightful fellow in company Iago was, and how natural it would be to like and trust him.

The audience has so far only seen him as a secret trouble-maker and may well be thinking 'why does Othello have such a man for his Ensign?' The scene in Cyprus gives a part of the answer.

He had been put in charge of Desdemona by Othello before they left Venice (I iii 285) and now, when she arrives with him in the midst of a tempest that has sunk the Turkish fleet, she is in deep anxiety for Othello's safety, which is still in doubt. It is Iago who rises to the occasion and steps forward to cheer and entertain her by the improvisation of a set of verses, tossed off on the spur of the moment, and as elegant as anything in *The Rape of the Lock*. It succeeds completely in taking Desdemona's mind off her worries and shows Iago's amusing social gifts, and care of a mistress entrusted to him. This is the reason for the little scene and therefore for the storm and the separation of man and wife. It has the further usefulness of leaving the audience in doubt whether or not the marriage of Othello and Desdemona has been consummated; for this will add sharpness to the second scene that demonstrates the kindly virtues of Iago.

Delightfulness is one thing, but honest-to-God good comradeship is another, and that is what we are next shown in him. That we may be certain it is sham, we first hear him priming Roderigo to stir up trouble against Cassio:

> *Cassio* knowes you not: Ile not be farre from you. Do you finde some occasion to anger *Cassio* ... he's rash, and very sodaine in Choller: and happely may strike at you, prouoke him that he may; for euen out of that will I cause these of Cyprus to Mutiny....
>
> (F II i 262–70)

We then see Iago, in all good fellowship, plying Cassio with drink, singing a rollicking song or two, with every appearance of high spirits and honest affection.

Roderigo plays his part; the pre-arranged fight takes place with a perfect spontaneity, nothing could seem more natural; uproar ensues, at the height of which Iago, decent fellow that he is, intervenes to prevent bloodshed:

> (*Iago*) Nay good Lieutenant. Alas Gentlemen:
> Helpe hoa. Lieutenant. Sir *Montano*:
> Helpe Masters. Here's a goodly Watch indeed.
>
> (F II iii 150–2)

and keeps it up until Othello, dragged by the riot from his wedding-bed, enters and demands the reason for it.

Nobody will tell him. At long last, and very reluctantly, Iago begins:

I had rather haue this tongue cut from my mouth,
Then it should do offence to *Michaell Cassio*.
Yet I perswade my selfe, to speake the truth
Shall nothing wrong him.... (F II iii 213–16)

What could be fairer, more honest, more convincingly friendly, more reliable and soldierly than Iago's behaviour, so far as Othello, Montana and even Cassio can think? And presently, after Othello has gone back to bed, it is Iago who consoles the stricken Cassio and advises him kindly and intelligently for his good. He only has to importune Desdemona to be reinstated, he tells him.

These two incidents – the storm and the brawl – establish Iago's honesty and kindness, and are the Siamese twins of his soliloquies, opposites that cannot be separated; there are other passages that show his manly delicacy, good faith and zeal:

I do beseech you,
Though I perchance am vicious in my guesse
(As I confesse it is my Natures plague
To spy into Abuses, and of* my iealousie
Shapes faults that are not) that your wisedome
From one, that so imperfectly conceits,
Would take no notice... (F III iii 148–54)

Such delicacy, such self-doubt, such eagerness for the peace of his master's mind, must convince anyone (who had not heard him in soliloquy) of Iago's honesty. In public he is as amiable and virtuous as Dr Jekyll; in soliloquy he shows us Mr Hyde.

Othello has one soliloquy that specially concerns us here; he needs it badly. He has to recreate the sympathy he has forfeited by striking his wife in public and by calling her 'that cunning whore of Venice' to her face. It would have been easy to have started the last scene – the scene of her murder – without a soliloquy. Desdemona need not have been asleep or even in bed, if

* [*read* oft]

Shakespeare had chosen to tell his story so. But the need for Othello to right himself with the audience before his murder of her, the need to show that he thought of it not as murder but as justice, was paramount; only by soliloquy could this be achieved.

Once again, as in the case of Brutus, the argument is over before the soliloquy begins; he has decided upon what to do, and what he says is the embroidery on that decision, not the argument that led him to it.

> It is the Cause, it is the Cause (my Soule)
> Let me not name it to you, you chaste Starres,
> It is the Cause. (F v ii 1–3)

Underlying the soliloquy of Brutus is the axiom that to seek a crown deserves death. Underlying that of Othello is the axiom that to commit adultery deserves death. Many men have held or acted on these axioms, and, in the theatre, we must accept them while we watch these plays; they are matters in which our disbelief must be suspended, for the sake of the other experiences we can derive from seeing them. Othello never questions the axiom that governs his action; his fault is folly, gullibility.

> O Foole, foole, foole! (v ii 326)

If the seeming-honesty of Iago, which we have discussed, is given full value in performance, Othello may still seem 'an honourable murderer'. The structure of the last scene is designed to help in this; it is symmetrically planned. It begins and ends in an attempt at an act of justice, on a kiss; and there is visual repetition too, for these acts are both placed on the wedding-death-bed of Desdemona and Othello. What more can be done by Othello to even out his fault than by paying for it in the same coin as he had made her pay? This is what the eye brings home to confirm what the ear hears in the opening soliloquy:

Oh Balmy breath, that dost almost perswade
Iustice to breake her Sword. One more, one more:
Be thus when thou art dead, and I will kill thee,
And loue thee after. One more, and that's the last.
(*He kisses her*. Q)
So sweet, was ne're so fatall. (F v ii 16–20)

On the same gesture the play finds its close:

I kist thee, ere I kill'd thee: No way but this,
Killing my selfe, to dye vpon a kisse.
(F v ii 361–2)

NOTES

1. Bernard Spivak, *Shakespeare and the Allegory of Evil* (Columbia, 1953).
2. This quotation comes from a newspaper report of Coleridge's lecture on *The Tempest* (1818).

SELECT BIBLIOGRAPHY

BOOKS

George R. Elliott, *Flaming Minister: A Study of Othello as Tragedy of Love and Hate* (Duke University Press, 1953). An interesting and deeply felt study of the play as a tragedy on the theme of pride. This, the chief of the deadly sins because it makes all the other sins inflexible, intermingles with love and causes it to be changed, at white-heat, to hate.

Robert B. Heilman, *Magic in the Web: Action and Language in 'Othello'* (University of Kentucky Press, 1956). A very detailed analysis – almost, at times, *too* exhaustive in its determination to cite all the evidence and leave no corner of the play unexamined, but full of good things, e.g. the best defence, if it needs one, of the apparent unrealism of Desdemona's return from death to utter her last words (pp. 215–16), or the brilliant analysis of Iago's 'Now I do love her too' soliloquy (pp. 200 ff.). Language, symbolism, theme, character – all are discussed, in conjunction and together, in a generously enthusiastic book that 'ne'er feels retiring ebb, but keeps due on'.

Marvin Rosenberg, *The Masks of Othello* (University of California Press, 1961). Subtitled 'The Search for the Identity of Othello, Iago and Desdemona by Three Centuries of Actors and Critics', this lively book gathers together what we know of the interpretations of these characters by great actors from the seventeenth century to the twentieth, and links them in a broad narrative fresco with the judgements of critics on these characters; it also offers a cogent statement of what Shakespearean interpretation owes, and must always owe, to the theatre.

Eldred Jones, *Othello's Countrymen: the African in English Renaissance Drama* (Oxford University Press for Fourah Bay College, 1965). By the middle of the sixteenth century, the English reader could learn about Africans from first-hand accounts as well as from Herodotus and other ancients. Africans (commonly called Moors) were frequent in the theatre; Mr Jones lists 45 dramatic works in which they appear, and describes many of the non-dramatic works from which playwrights probably took their material. Convention generally showed the Moor as villainous, like Shakespeare's early Aaron in *Titus Andronicus,* but sometimes allowed him the simpler kinds of nobility. Mr Jones compares Othello with Shakespeare's other Africans, and points out that it is Iago who 'reproduces and exaggerates many of the unfavourable characteristics commonly credited to Moors'. He deals also with the make-up and costume of Elizabethan stage Moors.

Shakespeare Survey, 21, ed. Kenneth Muir (Cambridge University Press, 1968). This issue of the annual *Survey* pays special attention to *Othello,* both in articles and illustrations. Particularly arresting is Ned B. Allen's study of the composition of the play, in which he argues that Shakespeare wrote Acts III, IV and V some time before he wrote I and II, so that many of the problems which have exercised critics are simply the result of inconsistencies between the first and second parts; Shakespeare 'made a play by splicing together two parts not originally written to go together'. Other contributors continue to treat *Othello* as a single play rather than two discrete fragments; Emrys Jones offers a useful sidelight in '*Othello,* "Lepanto" and the Cyprus Wars', which argues that the play is influenced by James I's heroic poem, 'Lepanto', especially in view of Shakespeare's position as chief dramatist to the 'King's Men'. Dame Helen Gardner contributes a terse but lucid survey of *Othello* criticism, 1900–67, while essays on Delacroix and Verdi illustrate the play's impact on the continental European sensibility.

ARTICLES

Lawrence J. Ross, 'Shakespeare's "Dull Clown" and Symbolic Music', in *Shakespeare Quarterly*, XVII (1966) 107–28. A study of the entry of the clown in III i. The dramatic function of this usually neglected scene is that it 'initiates the major movement of the play in which Iago has promised to untune the music of the hero and heroine's love'. Mr Ross cites, in support of this argument, the Platonic and Pythagorean concepts of musical harmony as a vital principle throughout the universe, and illustrates with many interesting reproductions from Renaissance visual art.

David Kaula, 'Othello Possessed: Notes on Shakespeare's Use of Magic and Witchcraft', in *Shakespeare Studies*, ed. Barroll (University of Cincinnati, 1966) pp. 112–32. This article assembles evidence about the contemporary state of opinion regarding witchcraft ('Shakespeare wrote *Othello* at a time when public anxiety in England over the possible dangers of witchcraft was more than usually intense'), and also argues that the theme of magic (e.g. in the handkerchief) is localized in certain scenes and does not become a major symbolic theme with reverberations throughout the play.

G. K. Hunter, '*Othello* and Colour Prejudice', in *Proceedings of the British Academy*, LIII (1967) 139–63. A most interesting treatment of the play in the light of Elizabethan attitudes towards colour, which Professor Hunter traces historically and relates to Shakespeare's treatment of both Othello and Iago. 'Shakespeare has presented to us a traditional view of what Moors are like, i.e. gross, disgusting, inferior, carrying the symbol of their damnation on their skin; and has caught our over-easy assent to such assumptions in the grip of a guilt which associates us and our assent with the white man representative of such views in the play – Iago. Othello acquires the glamour of an innocent man whom *we* have wronged, and an admiration stronger than he could have achieved by virtue plainly represented.'

NOTES ON CONTRIBUTORS

W. H. AUDEN (1907–73). English-born poet: took American citizenship in 1941. Widely influential since first book, *Poems* (1930). Much criticism, notably *The Dyer's Hand* (1963). Professor of Poetry at Oxford 1956–61.

JOHN BAYLEY. Novelist and critic; Thomas Wharton Professor of English Literature, University of Oxford. His critical studies include *The Romantic Survival* (1957), *Characters of Love* (1961) and *The Uses of Division: Unity and Disharmony in Literature* (1976).

A. C. BRADLEY (1851–1935). English critic. Taught at the universities of Oxford, Liverpool and Glasgow; Professor of Poetry at Oxford, 1901–6.

NEVILL COGHILL. (1899—1980) critic, producer, teacher. Oxford don (was Auden's tutor), preceded Dame Helen Gardner as Merton Professor of English Language and Literature. Much theatrical work, including co-authorship of successful adaptation from Chaucer, *The Canterbury Tales* (1968). Books include *Geoffrey Chaucer* (1966) and *Shakespeare's Professional Skills* (1964).

T. S. ELIOT (1888–1965). Major poet and critic. American-born, settled in England in 1915 and took British nationality in 1927. Nobel Prize for Literature, 1948.

WILLIAM EMPSON. Poet and critic; Professor Emeritus of English, University of Sheffield. His critical studies include *Seven Types of Ambiguity* (1930), *Some Versions of Pastoral* (1935) and *The Structure of Complex Words* (1951).

DAME HELEN GARDNER. Critic and editor; Professor Emeritus of English, University of Oxford. Her publications include *The Business of Criticism* (1960), important work on Donne, Milton and T.S. Eliot and the new version of the *Oxford Book of English Verse*.

G. Wilson Knight. Critic, producer, actor and teacher; Professor Emeritus of English, University of Leeds. He pioneered modern Shakespearean criticism with *Myth and Miracle* (1929), *The Wheel of Fire* (1930), *The Imperial Theme* (1931), *The Shakespearean Tempest* (1932; 1953), *Shakespearean Production* (1936; 1964) and *The Crown of Life* (1947). He is the foremost exponent of the symbolic interpretation of Shakespeare.

F. R. Leavis (1895–1978). Critic and educationalist; taught at Cambridge and was co-founder and editor of the influential review *Scrutiny* (1932–53). His publications include *The Great Tradition* (1948), *English Literature* in *Our time and the University* (1969), *Never Shall My Sword* (1972), *The Living Principle* (1975) and *Thoughts, Words and Creativity* (1976).

INDEX